True Border

D1711185

100 Questions and Answers about the U.S.-Mexico Frontera

Borderzine

El Paso, Texas

To learn more about this book and the authors, please visit www.Borderzine.com.

Published by
Borderzine
500 W. University Ave.
El Paso, Texas

Cover design and illustration by Roger Fidler.

Front cover photo by Stella Chavez/KERA.

Front Edge Publishing books are available for discount bulk purchases for events, corporate use and small groups. Special editions, including books with corporate logos, personalized covers and customized interiors are available for purchase. For more information, contact Front Edge Publishing at info@ FrontEdgePublishing.com.

Contents

The Border: A Double Sonnet

by Alberto Ríos

The border is a line that birds cannot see.

The border is a beautiful piece of paper folded carelessly in half.

The border is where flint first met steel, starting a century of fires.

The border is a belt that is too tight, holding things up but making it hard to breathe.

The border is a rusted hinge that does not bend.

The border is the blood clot in the river's vein.

The border says *stop* to the wind, but the wind speaks another language, and keeps going.

The border is a brand, the "Double-X" of barbed wire scarred into the skin of so many.

The border has always been a welcome stopping place but is now a stop sign, always red.

The border is a jump rope still there even after the game is finished.

The border is a real crack in an imaginary dam.

The border used to be an actual place, but now, it is the act of a thousand imaginations.

The border, the word *border*, sounds like *order*, but in this place they do not rhyme.

The border is a handshake that becomes a squeezing contest.

The border smells like cars at noon and wood smoke in the evening.

The border is the place between the two pages in a book where the spine is bent too far.

The border is two men in love with the same woman.

The border is an equation in search of an equals sign.

The border is the location of the factory where lightning and thunder are made.

The border is "NoNo" The Clown, who can't make anyone laugh.

The border is a locked door that has been promoted.

The border is a moat but without a castle on either side.

The border has become Checkpoint *Chale.*

The border is a place of plans constantly broken and repaired and broken.

The border is mighty, but even the parting of the seas created a path, not a barrier.

The border is a big, neat, clean, clear black line on a map that does not exist.

The border is the line in new bifocals: below, small things get bigger; above, nothing changes.

The border is a skunk with a white line down its back.

Acknowledgements and credits

The following contributed to the reporting, writing, editing and visuals for Borderzine's **Our Border Life** project.

Dino Chiecchi, ebook editor and photographer

Zita Arocha, project director

Kate Gannon, digital editor and English podcasting

Monica Ortiz Uribe, Spanish podcasting

Joe Grimm, project advisor

Roger Fidler, covers graphic design

Stella Chavez/KERA, cover photo

Shelley Armitage, writer

David Smith-Soto, copy editor

Myriam Cruz, translator

Roberto Perez Diaz, translator

Dr. Eva Moya, cross border survey

Dr. Josiah Heyman, cross border survey

Mario Porras, cross border survey

Universidad Autónoma de Ciudad Juarez, collaborator

Rocio Gallegos, La Verdad

Gabriela Minjáres, La Verdad

Front Edge Publishing

Trish Long

Tim Archuleta

A special thank you to Online News Association for its generous support of Borderzine's Our Border Life project and this ebook.

Student reporters

Jacqueline Aguirre

Kevin Ceniceros

Marisol S. Chavez

Juan Corral

Lucero Fierro

Richard Gonzalez

Daniel Gonzalez

Jessica Leal

Tracy Martinez

Alexia Nava

Valeria Olivares

Denisse Santiesteban-Villegas

Valeria Santos

Leslie Sariñana
Mariana Sierra
Genaro Soriano
Ruben Soto
Fabiola Terrazas
Samantha Turley
Paulette Villa
UACJ students

Interviews with local residents
Gilbert Anaya
Nuria Andreu
Adrian Aragones
Elvira Carrizal-Dukes
S. Cassandro
Dino Chiecchi
Dr. Irasema Coronado
Myriam Cruz
Angelica Denton
Kerry Doyle
Maria D. Hermosillo
Raquel Hernandez
Dr. Miguel Juarez
Robert E. Mosher
Sito Negron
Eugenia Posada

Vanesa Reimers
Patrick Schaefer
Sally Spener
Antonio Villa Alcazar
Diana Washington Valdez

Photographers
Celeste Gomez
Aaron Martinez
Stephanie Salazar
Miguel Contreras
Will Seyffert
Ruben R. Ramirez
Mark Lambie
Rudy Gutierrez
Victor Calzada
Vanessa Monsisvais
Leslie Sarinana
Dino Chiecchi

Preface

Like many great ideas, the germ for this book came
from a conversation.

University of Texas at El Paso Assistant Professor
Maria de los Angeles Flores ran into Michigan State
University visiting editor in residence Joe Grimm at
a conference and they began talking about a series
of books Grimm had created called Bias Busters.
The books, in Q&A format, seek to dispel common
misconceptions about racial and ethnic communities,
cultures, religions and pressing social issues in the U.S.

Flores returned to campus, shared the conversation
with Borderzine staff and shortly after a lengthy phone
call with Grimm, we began production for a bilingual
binational digital project called "Engaging Community
Across Borders through Media."

Funded by a grant from the Online News
Association, the project includes this ebook, an
accompanying series of podcasts and multimedia
storytelling on Borderzine by student journalists from
UTEP and the Universidad Autónoma de Ciudad
Juarez.

Borderzine.com turned 10 last year and is a journalism-based student-produced bilingual website professionally edited and managed by multimedia journalist professors at UTEP.

In spring 2018, we created an upper-division elective class and 10 students began to work with me on identifying 10 chapter topics, doing preliminary research and interviewing more than a dozen border experts and community members. Another class formed in spring 2019, headed by Associate Professor Dino Chiecchi, and another 10 students completed the research and began some of the editing.

While Chiecchi and his team worked on the book, Associate Professor Kate Gannon began production of a special web page on the Borderzine website called "My Border Life," and, with support from radio journalist Monica Ortiz Uribe, began to produce the podcast conversations with residents from both sides of the borderline.

Chiecchi edited the book during summer 2019, and it was then shipped to translators for a Spanish-language version that accompanies the English version of the book. Former Knight-Ridder Executive Roger Fidler volunteered to design the front and back covers of the book, and former Borderzine professor David Smith-Soto provided final copyediting. A complete list of contributors is on the credits page.

"True Border," the 17th in the Bias Busters series, was published in January 2020 and the accompanying web site was launched at the same time, to include "Our Border Life" podcasts, multimedia stories and photo galleries for each chapter.

Our intention from the start was to explain, provide context for and go beyond the prevalent stereotypes and misperceptions many people have about the unique, vibrant, and culturally rich 2000-mile zone that more than 20 million call home.

We hope you agree we have accomplished that.

Adelante,

Zita Arocha

Introduction

A friend of mine once told me that the U.S.-Mexico border is a land unto itself. It is neither part of the U.S. nor part of Mexico.

That 20-mile stretch of land north of the border, and in Texas north of the Rio Grande, and the 20 miles south of the borderline are a place unique and unlike any place in either country. The U.S. starts 20 miles north of the border and Mexico starts some 20 miles south. That 40-mile swath—20 miles on either side of the nearly 2,000-mile long border—is special because its people are special.

Two languages are spoken, and sometimes within the same sentence. A recent survey showed a large percentage of non-Hispanic U.S. residents have decided to learn Spanish, and a smaller percentage but a still sizable number of Mexicans learn English. Cash registers in Ciudad Juarez, for example, often have as many American greenbacks in their tills as they do pesos. Not so much on the U.S. side, but many businesses do accept pesos sometimes to the dislike of their farther north American cousins.

Celebrations like Dia de Los Muertos, which commemorates loved ones who have departed, is a quintessential Mexican holiday. But Americans are starting to celebrate it with gusto. San Antonio just celebrated its first Dia los Muertos river parade along the famed River Walk. Halloween has been a childhood fascination in Mexico for years, and Thanksgiving—that American celebration of the Pilgrims after their first harvest in 1621—is being more widely accepted in Mexico as dia de las gracias.

The U.S.-Mexico border is essential to both countries as their cultures intermingle and commerce continues to grow, first with the advent of the North American Free Trade Agreement in 1994 and now its apparent replacement—the United States-Mexico-Canada Agreement, which is pending ratification. Billions of dollars worth of products cross the border each year, and millions of people either walk or drive across the border annually.

The relationship between the two countries, and that special land that separates yet joins the nations, is essential for the pulse of the nations and its people are inexorably linked.

Dino Chiecchi

Editor

Associate Professor

University of Texas at El Paso

A Folklorico dancer performs at El Paso's San Jacinto Plaza. Photo by El Paso Times.

Legendary Mexican singer Juan Gabriel performs in the Don Haskins Center before a sold-out concert on Feb. 18, 2015. Juan Gabriel was welcomed with a thunderous standing ovation as he walked in via stage left. Photo by Ruben Ramirez/El Paso Times.

Identity and Border Language

What is the preferred term to identify someone who is in the U.S. without documentation?

The term is undocumented, as opposed to documented. The Merriam-Webster dictionary identifies undocumented as:

1: not supported by documentary evidence

- undocumented expenditures

2: lacking documents required for legal immigration or residence

- undocumented workers

Why are immigrants often referred to as illegal aliens?

Alien is derived from the Latin term *alienus*, meaning "foreigner" or "outsider." The term was first used in immigration applications going back to the 1950s or earlier. It is considered pejorative.

What is a fronterizo?[1]A Borderlander?

Fronterizo can be defined as someone from the frontier, or someone who has a relation with the border between states. The term can also refer to a place that has a common border with another place.

What does Hispanic[2] mean?

Hispanic refers to someone who is a native of, or descends from, a Spanish-speaking country. The term Hispano/Hispana (Hispanic) wasn't invented in the U.S. It's a Spanish word that means belonging or relating to Hispania (Spain and Portugal), and belonging or relating to Hispanoamérica (countries in the Americas where Spanish is spoken). Hispanic came into use officially in the U.S. in the early 1970s during the Richard Nixon presidency. The U.S. government decided to adopt Hispanic as a universal term that could serve to include all Spanish-speaking groups in the U.S. Typically, a person born in Spain or who descends from Spain is referred to as Spanish or a Spaniard.

---

1 https://www.lexico.com/es/definicion/fronterizo
2 https://www.exploratorium.edu/sites/default/files/
Genial_2017_Terms_of_Usage.pdf

Who are Chicano/Chicanas?[3]

A Chicano/Chicana is someone who is native of, or descends from, Mexico and who lives in the U.S. Chicano or Chicana is a chosen identity of some Mexican Americans in the U.S. The term became widely used during the Chicano Movement of the 1960s by many Mexican Americans to express a political stance founded on pride in a shared cultural, ethnic, and community identity.

What are low-riders, cholos and pachucos?

A low-rider is a customized vehicle with hydraulic jacks that allow the chassis to be lowered nearly to the road. Low-riders are common around El Paso. There are a large number of car clubs in El Paso that consist of low-riders. These car clubs gather on Sundays for car shows. The shows include other vehicles as well. The low-rider trend began in Southern California in the 1950s and early 1960s. The peak of the infamous low-rider trend in the Borderlands hit Los Angeles in the 1970s.[4]

Cholos and pachucos are also well known within the low-rider community. Cholos in the Borderland can be depicted as Latin and Mexican American communities that may or may not be associated with a street gang. A pachuco is a Mexican American who may or may not be associated with a gang, and their

3 https://www.exploratorium.edu/sites/default/files/ Genial_2017_Terms_of_Usage.pdf

4 http://www.historyaccess.com/historyoflowride.html

styles are both different. Cholos may dress in certain colors, royal or navy blue, and khakis. Pachucos normally dress down, with suspenders, a tie and a button up.

What does Latino/Latina mean?

Latino/Latina refers to someone who is native of, or descends from, a Latin country. The term Latino/Latina includes people from Brazil and excludes those who were born in Spain. Not all Brazilians identify themselves as Latino/Latina, but many do. Thus, Hispanic refers more to language, while Latino/Latina refers more to culture.

What does Latinx mean?

Latinx is a gender-neutral term to refer to a Latino/Latina person. The "x" replaces the male and female endings "o" and "a" that are part of Spanish grammar conventions. This term comes from American-born Latinos/Latinas who want to be more inclusive and gender-neutral, which is more akin to the English language.

Who are Mexican Americans?

A Mexican American is a citizen or resident of the U.S. of Mexican birth or descent.

Who are Anglos?

An Anglo is a white American of non-Hispanic descent, distinguished especially from an American of Mexican or Spanish descent. An Anglo also can be an English-speaking person in a place where English is not the language of the majority.

What is a gringo?[5] Where does the term come from?

The etymology or origin of the Spanish word is uncertain, although it is likely to have come from griego, the word for "Greek." In Spanish, as in English, it has long been common to refer to an unintelligible language as Greek. Over time, griego's apparent variant, gringo, came to refer to a foreign language and to foreigners in general. The first known written English use of the word was in 1849 by an explorer.

Folk etymology regarding gringo indicates that it originated in Mexico during the Mexican American War because Americans would sing the song "Green Grow the Lilies." As the word originated in Spain long before there was a Spanish-speaking Mexico, there is no truth to this urban legend. In fact, at one time, the word in Spanish was often used to refer specifically to the Irish. And according to a 1787 dictionary, it often referred to someone who spoke Spanish poorly.

---

5 https://www.thoughtco.com/gringo-in-spanish-3080284

In both English and Spanish, gringa is used to refer to a female. In Spanish, the term

Gringolandia is sometimes used to refer to the U.S. Gringolandia can also refer to the tourist zones of some Spanish-speaking countries, especially those areas where many Americans congregate. Another related word is engringarse, to act like a gringo. Although the word appears in dictionaries, it doesn't appear to have much actual use.

Who does paisano refer to?

A paisano is a countryman, a compatriot. The term also used to refer to a friend or pal.

What is a Dreamer?[6]

A Dreamer (often also spelled "DREAMer") refers to a young person who qualifies for the Development, Relief, and Education for Alien Minors (DREAM) Act in the context of immigration reform. Dreamers are also frequently referred to as "DACA recipients," though the latter specifically refers to Dreamers who have applied for and received DACA status. While the majority of Dreamers are Latino, they are a diverse group and come from a multitude of countries and cultures. Seven of the top 24 countries for Dreamers are in Asia, Europe, or the Caribbean. Tens of thousands of young Dreamers come from South Korea, the Philippines, India, Jamaica, Tobago, Poland, Nigeria, Pakistan, Brazil, the Dominican Republic and Guyana.

6 https://americasvoice.org/blog/what-is-a-dreamer/

What does Pachuco[7] mean?

Pachuco refers to a Mexican American youth subculture. The pachuco subculture arose from the social issues Mexican American youth experienced during the later decades of the 19th century and early decades of the 20th century. The cultural practices of the pachuco developed through a complex interaction between the Mexican American youths and their experiences in a dominant culture. Media reports frequently classified these Mexican American youths as unpatriotic delinquents destroying American cities. The Chicano movement later took up many of the pachuco core beliefs and meanings as the pachuco subculture faded during the 1950s.

What does cholo mean?

The term cholo can refer to people of indigenous or partly indigenous ancestry. In the U.S., it can refer to a young man belonging to a Mexican American urban subculture associated with street gangs.

What is a fresa?[8]

A fresa is a strawberry, but in Mexico it can refer to someone who is snobby or generally well off, too.

---

7 https://haenfler.sites.grinnell.edu/subcultures-and-scenes/pachuco/
8 https://theculturetrip.com/north-america/mexico/articles/all-the-mexican-slang-terms-you-need-to-know/

What is machismo?

The term machismo can refer to a strong sense of masculine pride. It can also express sexism or misogyny.

Socorro Mission in Socorro, Texas.
Photo by Aaron Martinez.

Mount Cristo Rey on the U.S.-Mexico
border. Photo by Will Seyffert.

Religion, Culture and Social Justice

What are the common religions practiced in the Borderlands?

The most recent study done in 2010 by The Association of Religious Data Archives shows there are about 350,000 residents of the El Paso area who identify as Catholic, or 43.2%. The same area includes about 51,000 residents who identify as Evangelical Protestant. About 16% of Arizona residents identify as Catholic. Many of the border regions, including California, Arizona, Texas and New Mexico, are predominantly Catholic. About 29% of California residents and 29% of New Mexico residents identify as Catholic.[9][10]

---

9 http://www.city-data.com/county/El_Paso_County-TX.html
10 https://www.nytimes.com/2014/10/26/us/catholics-in-el-paso-could-set-the-tone.html

Who is la Virgen de Guadalupe?

La Virgen de Guadalupe, also known as the Virgin of Guadalupe, is highly celebrated by Catholics in Mexico with a feast. She is also known as "La Reina de México." The Virgin of Guadalupe is celebrated because of the belief that a farmer named Juan Diego encountered the Virgin of Guadalupe on Dec. 12, 1531. Juan Diego is also a saint highly regarded in Mexico, who, according to tradition, visited the Virgin of Guadalupe. The Virgin of Guadalupe represents many things in the Mexican culture, from motherhood to ecological justice.[11]

What is Day of the Dead and why is it celebrated?

The Day of the Dead, in Mexico known as "Dia de los Muertos," is a celebration of those who died. Family and friends are celebrated, and those that celebrate take possessions to graves and honor the dead. Many of the residents in the Borderlands celebrate Halloween and Dia de Los Muertos.
Dia de los Muertos is a Catholic holiday celebrated along with All Saints Day and All Souls day, Nov. 1 and Nov. 2, respectively. All Saints Day celebrates Catholic saints and All Souls Day represents the souls of the dead within the faith. Shrines are set up with photographs of the deceased, along with some of their favorite foods and items so that the living may celebrate with the dead once more.

---

11 https://www.latinlife.com/article/61/
la-virgen-de-guadalupe-history

What is a posada and how is it celebrated?

A posada is a nine day Catholic festival that commemorates the journey of Mary and Joseph from Nazareth to Bethlehem. Each day of the festival children lead a procession through the streets of town dressed as Mary and Joseph holding candles, seeking shelter. A Catholic Mass is held every night of the festival, followed by a celebration during which children break piñatas and music is played. The celebration is best known for its traditional Mexican foods like pozole, tamales, a hot punch-like drink called "ponche," and fried buñuelos. The posada runs from Dec. 16 to 24 so that the last Mass is held at midnight to welcome the birth of Jesus. In Mexican culture, Christmas celebrations begin with the final day of posada.

What is a mission?

Catholic beginnings on the border are symbolized by missions that were established by Spanish settlers in the early 17th century as religious centers and forts during war. Three of the oldest historic missions are located along the El Paso border region. The three missions are the Ysleta Mission, Socorro Mission and San Elizario Mission. All three missions are still open and functioning today. These three missions connect Hispanics and Native Americans of the region culturally. The Ysleta Mission stands in the middle of Native Tigua land, where it has stood since 1692. The San Elizario Mission was created to serve as a fort for Mexican troops in the Mission Valley. The Socorro Mission was created as refuge for Spanish colonizers in 1680, according to the Catholic Diocese of El Paso. The exterior design of the missions was influential on the New Mexico architecture that exists today.[12]

What are sanctuary cities?

Sanctuary cities exist in the U.S. as cities that protect immigrants by limiting the power of law enforcement and federal agencies, such as the U.S. Immigration and Customs Enforcement (ICE). Often, the purpose of these cities is misinterpreted; they do not exist to harbor fugitives or immigrants, but to protect immigrants from facing deportation and breaking up their families as well as to encourage them to report crimes and use social services. In Texas, there are no sanctuary cities as a result of Senate Bill 4, passed in 2017, that bans sanctuary cities. According to a data from a study by the Center for Immigration Studies, the only sanctuary cities along the U.S.-Mexico border are San Miguel, N.M. and San Diego, Calif. New Mexico and California are also the only states along the border that have sanctuary cities.[13]

Who are the Tohono O'odham?

The Borderlands are not only made up of Mexican people, but also indigenous people who have lived

12 https://www.elpasodiocese.org/historic-missions.html
13 https://cis.org/Map-Sanctuary-Cities-Counties-and-States

along the border long before the border divisions even existed. The Tohono O'odham, who comprise around 32,000 citizens, are based across all of Arizona and near the Sonora border, where they own desert lands. For years, the O'odham have lived harmoniously, crossing between the U.S. and Mexico through their own land, but their way of living has become interrupted by borders and increased border security, forcing them to travel longer distances in order to cross through a designated port of entry rather than through any passage on their land, as they are allowed to do. This particular nation is unique to the border because border lines have divided their people into two different countries. Vice chairman for the O'odham Nation, Verlon Jose, has spoken publicly about their opposition to a border wall, as the border division could stop them from being able to cross through their land at all. The tribe also has expressed that the division has left some Native Americans feeling detached from their relatives in Mexico.

Are there other Native American groups along the border?

According to the Native American Environmental Protection Coalition, there are 24 Native American tribes along the U.S.-Mexico border that exist in the U.S. and five that exist in Mexico.

The Arizona Border Tribes:

Cocopah, Pascua Yaqui, Quechan and Tohono O'odham.

California Border Tribes:

Barona Band of Mission Indians, Campo Kumeyaay Nation, Ewiaapaayp Band of Kumeyaay, Indians, Inaja-Cosmit Band of Mission Indians, Jamul Indian Village, La Jolla Band of Luiseno, La Posta Band of Mission Indians, Los Coyotes Band of Cahuilla and Cupeno Indians, Manzanita Band of Kumeyaay Nation, Mesa Grande Band Of Indians, Pala Band of Mission Indians, Pauma Band of Mission Indians, Pechanga Band of Luiseno Indians, Rincon Band of Luiseno Indians, San Pasqual Band of Mission Indians, Iipay Nation of Santa Ysabel, Sycuan, Band of the Kumeyaay Nation and Viejas Band of the Kumeyaay Indians.

Texas Border Tribes:

Kickapoo Traditional Tribe of Texas and Ysleta Del Sur Pueblo.

New Mexico Native American Tribes:

There are 23 indigenous tribes in the state of New Mexico. Of these, 19 are Pueblos, three are Apache (Fort Sill Apache Tribe, Jicarilla Apache Nation, Mescalero Apache Tribe), and the Navajo Nation.

The 19 Pueblos are: Acoma, Cochiti, Isleta, Jemez, Laguna, Nambe, OhKay, Owingeh, Picuris, Pojoaque, Sandia, San Felipe, San Ildefonso, Santa Ana, Santa Clara, Santo Domingo, Taos, Tesuque, Zuni and Zia.

Indigenous Communities of Mexico include:

Cucapa (Cocopah), Kikapu (Kickapoo), Kumiai (Kumeyaay), Paipai and San Francisquito (Tohono O'odham).

What is the Charity Network?

The Charity Navigator is a nonprofit organization that helps people who are looking to give back by providing data on finances, accountability and transparency of charities in the U.S. Residents of the Borderlands are not strangers to giving back, as many area residents often donate food, clothes or blankets to organizations that take those items to people in need, across the border into Mexico. People who are looking for organizations to donate through or just want more information on specific organizations can go to Charity Network and also make donations through them. The network has information on more than 9,000 charities across the country. Each year, donations made through them have increased. According to Guide Star, the Charity Navigator made more than $23 million in donations, which came directly through their website in 2018, a $9 million increase from the donations made in 2017.[14][15]

14 https://www.charitynavigator.org/index.cfm?bay=content.
view&cpid=628
15 https://www.guidestar.org/profile/13-4148824

Border Patrol Agent in Charge Eagle Pass, Bryan Kemmett, left, passes a seven year old boy from Honduras to another agent after he was rescued from the swollen Rio Grande River. Agents responded to three rafts crossing the river in Eagle Pass, on Friday, May 10, 2019. A total of 9 were helped out of the river.

Thousands of cars cross from Ciudad Juarez to El Paso at the Sante Fe bridge early in the morning. Photo by Dino Chiecchi.

Border Crossings

What are CBP and ICE? What do they do?

The security of the border is divided into three organizations:

> Immigration benefits - USCIS
> Immigration enforcement- ICE
> Immigration inspection - CBP

U.S. Customs and Border Protection is a component of the Department of Homeland Security. It has the primary responsibility of securing the nation's borders. The U.S. Border Patrol is the uniformed enforcement division of CBP responsible for border security between designated official ports of entry into the country. The Border Patrol's mission since the Sept. 11 terrorist attacks has been to prevent terrorists and terrorist weapons from entering the U.S. between official ports of entry. In addition, the Border Patrol has a traditional mission of preventing undocumented immigrants, smugglers, narcotics and other contraband from entering the country.

Border Patrol agents generally report to Border Patrol stations and substations in each of these sectors. These stations function much as police stations do for police personnel around the country. The number of stations and substations varies widely by sector.[16]

Where are the border checkpoints and what do they do?

Here is a list of border checkpoints:

California

- San Clemente: 7 miles south of San Clemente on Interstate 5.
- Temecula: 24 miles north of Escondido on Interstate 15.
- Highway 79: 1 mile west of Sunshine Summit.
- Interstate 8 West: 3 miles east of Pine Valley on Interstate 8.
- Highway 94: 24 miles east of San Diego on California State Route 94.
- Highway 78/86: just south of the intersection of California State Routes 78 and 86, just west of the Salton Sea, controlling northbound traffic only.
- Highway 111: between Niland and Bombay Beach.
- Highway S2: 7 miles north of Ocotillo and I-8 in eastern San Diego County on S2 (Imperial Hwy/Sweeney Pass Road) between I-8 and State Route 78.

---

16 https://www.cbp.gov/border-security/along-us-borders/overview

Arizona

- I-8 (eastbound only): 15 miles east of Yuma on Interstate 8.
- I-19: northbound from Nogales just north of Tubac.
- Arivaca Road: northeast through Amado, located near mile marker 22.
- Ariz. Hwy 286: northbound from Sasabe to Three Points.
- Ariz. Hwy 86: eastbound off the Tohono O'odham reservation, before three points.
- Indian Highway 15 North of Sells near Kahatk.
- Ariz. Hwy 90: northbound from Whetstone to Benson.
- Ariz. Hwy 80: northbound from Tombstone to Benson (at junction with AZ 82 west).
- U.S. Hwy 95: northbound from Yuma to Quartzsite, 53.4 miles north of Yuma.
- Ariz. Hwy 85: 0.7 miles south of Why.
- Ariz. Hwy 85: 18.4 miles south of Gila Bend.

New Mexico

- I-10 West: 22 miles west of Las Cruces on Interstate 10, between mile markers 120-121.
- I-25 North: 23 miles north of Las Cruces on Interstate 25.
- U.S. 70 East: 15 miles southwest of Alamogordo on U.S. Route 70, between mile markers 198-199.
- Alamogordo: 30 miles south of Alamogordo on U.S. Route 54, between mile markers 40-41.

- N.M. Highway 11: 22.6 miles south of Deming on N.M. Hwy 11, between mile markers 12-13.
- N.M. Highway 185: 13 miles northwest of Radium Springs on N.M. Hwy 185, between mile markers 25-26.

Texas

- U.S. Route 62: 33 miles east of El Paso.
- Sierra Blanca: between El Paso and Van Horn, 5 miles west of Sierra Blanca on Interstate 10.
- Eagle Pass: 11 miles east of Eagle Pass on U.S. Route 57.
- Eagle Pass/Carrizo Springs: 30 miles west-southwest of Eagle Pass on U.S. Route 277.
- Brackettville/Uvalde: 60 miles east of Del Rio, Texas on Highway 90.
- Laredo: 29 miles north of Laredo on Interstate 35.
- Laredo 83: 35 miles north of Laredo on Highway 83.
- Freer: 16 miles west of Freer on U.S. Route 59.
- Oilton: 6 miles east of Oilton on Highway 359.
- Falfurias: 14 miles south of Falfurrias on U.S. Highway 281.
- Sarita: 14 miles south of Sarita on U.S. Route 77.
- Hebbronville: 1 mile south of Hebbronville on Texas 16 S.
- Hebbronville: 50 yards south on FM 1017 at "T" intersection of Highway 285.

- Alpine: 10 miles south of Alpine on Texas State Highway 118.
- Brownsville: on Boca Chica Highway leading to Boca Chica Beach.
- Marfa: 4.5 miles south of Marfa on U.S. Route 67.

Source: https://www.gao.gov/new.items/d05435.pdf

The interior and border checkpoints are permanent. Tactical interior traffic checkpoints are generally located on major and secondary roads, usually 25 to 75 miles inland from the border.

Why are the Border Patrol uniforms green?

After the Sept. 11 terror attacks, former President George W. Bush assured the public of more secure borders to prevent terrorists coming to the U.S. CBP was established on March 1, 2003, according to Melinda Lauck, a criminal justice department lecturer at the University of Texas at El Paso. There is no reason why the Border Patrol wears green uniforms specifically, but over the years the olive green color has helped to differentiate CBP officers from Border Patrol officers.

How has Border Patrol and CBP grown over the last 20 years?

Prior to the terror attacks, border security was in hands of many government agencies. Creating the CBP placed that responsibility under one organization.

CPB Through the Years

The Origins of the Border Patrol

Mounted agents of the U.S. Immigration Service patrolled the border to prevent illegal crossings as early as 1904, but their efforts were irregular and undertaken only when resources permitted. The inspectors, usually called mounted guards, operated out of El Paso. Though they never totaled more than 75, they patrolled as far west as California, trying to restrict the flow of illegal Chinese immigration.

In March 1915, Congress authorized a separate group of mounted guards, often referred to as mounted inspectors. Most rode on horseback, but a few operated cars and even boats. Although these inspectors had broader arrest authority, they still largely pursued Chinese immigrants trying to avoid Chinese exclusion laws.

Texas Rangers were also sporadically assigned to patrol duties by the state, and their efforts were noted as "singularly effective."

Prohibition and Border Control

The 18th Amendment to the U.S. Constitution, prohibiting the importation, transport, manufacture or sale of alcoholic beverages went into effect Jan. 16, 1920. With the passage of this constitutional amendment and the numerical limits placed on immigration to the U.S. by the Immigration Acts of 1921 and 1924, border enforcement received renewed attention from the government. The numerical limitations forced immigrants from around the world to try illegal entry if attempts to enter legally failed. Therefore, the mission of the Border Patrol became more important to the U.S. government.

These events set change into motion. On May 28, 1924, Congress passed the Labor Appropriation Act of 1924, officially establishing the U.S. Border Patrol for the purpose of securing the borders between inspection stations. In 1925, its duties were expanded to patrol the sea coast.

The Beginning

Officers were quickly recruited for the new positions. The Border Patrol expanded to 450 officers. Many of the early agents were recruited from organizations like the Texas Rangers, local sheriffs and deputies and appointees from the Civil Service Register of Railroad Mail Clerks.

Recruits furnished their own horse and saddle, but Washington supplied oats and hay for the horses and a $1,680 annual salary for the agents. The agents did not wear uniforms until 1928.

In 1932, the Border Patrol was placed under the authority of two directors, one in charge of the Mexican border office in El Paso, the other in charge of the Canadian border office in Detroit. Liquor smuggling was a major concern because it too often accompanied alien smuggling. The majority of the Border Patrol was assigned to the Canadian border. Smuggling was also commonplace along the Mexican border. Whiskey bootleggers avoided the bridges and slipped their cargo across the Rio Grande on pack mules.

The first Border Patrol Academy opened as a training school at Camp Chigas, El Paso, in December 1934. Thirty-four trainees attended classes in marksmanship and horsemanship.

Although horses remained the transportation of choice for many years, by 1935 the Border Patrol began using motorized vehicles equipped with radios. Rugged terrain and the need for quick, quiet transportation guaranteed that horses would remain essential transportation to the Patrol even to the present day.

During the War

The workload and accomplishments of the Border Patrol remained fairly constant until 1940, when the Immigration Service was moved from the Department of Labor to the Department of Justice. An additional 712 agents and 57 auxiliary personnel brought the force to 1,531 officers. Over 1,400 people were employed by the Border Patrol in law enforcement and civilian positions by the end of WW II. During the war, the patrol provided tighter control of the border, staffed detention camps, guarded diplomats and assisted the U.S. Coast Guard in searching for Axis saboteurs. Aircraft proved extremely effective and became an integral part of operations.

Border Patrol Role Expands

Legislation in 1952 codified and carried forward the essential elements of the 1917 and 1924 acts. The same year, Border Patrol agents were first permitted to board and search a conveyance for illegal immigrants anywhere in the U.S. For the first time, illegal entrants traveling within the country were subject to arrest.

As illegal immigration continued along the Mexican border, 62 Canadian border units were transferred south for a large-scale repatriation effort. In 1952, the government airlifted 52,000 illegal immigrants back to the Mexican interior. The program was terminated after it ran out of funds during its first year. The Mexican government offered train rides into the Mexican interior for nationals being returned from the San Antonio and Los Angeles districts, but this program was halted after only five months. Throughout the early 1950s, a special taskforce of 800 Border Patrol agents was assigned by the U.S. attorney general to round up and ship home thousands of illegal immigrants in southern California. The task force moved to the Lower Rio Grande Valley, then to Chicago and other interior cities. The Border Patrol began expelling adult Mexican males by boatlift from Port Isabel, Texas, to Vera Cruz in September 1954. The project was discontinued two years later after nearly 50,000 undocumented immigrants had been returned home. Various other flights, train trips, and bus trips originated along the border and terminated in the Mexican interior. Despite the major successes in repatriation, many deportees simply turned around and again crossed the seriously undermanned border. Repatriation programs proved expensive and were phased out primarily because of cost.

Significant numbers of undocumented immigrants began entering the U.S. on private aircraft in the late 1950s. In cooperation with other federal services, the Border Patrol began tracking suspect flights. During the Cuban missile crisis of the early 1960s, Cuban defectors living in Florida flew aircraft out over the ocean in an effort to harass their former homeland. The American government made this harassment illegal, and assigned the Border Patrol to prevent unauthorized flights. The patrol added 155 officers, but discharged 122 of them when the crisis ended in 1963.

The early 1960s also witnessed aircraft-hijacking attempts. President John F. Kennedy ordered Border Patrol agents to accompany domestic flights to prevent takeovers. The Miami sector of the Border Patrol coordinated the effort. Immigrant smuggling eventually evolved to drug smuggling. The Border Patrol assisted other agencies in intercepting illegal drugs from Mexico.

Today's Border Patrol

The 1980s and 1990s saw a tremendous increase of illegal migration to America. The Border Patrol responded with increases in manpower and the implementation of modern technology. Infrared night-vision scopes, seismic sensors and a modern computer processing system helped the Border Patrol locate, apprehend and process those crossing into the U.S. illegally.

In an effort to bring a level of control to the border, Operation Hold the Line was established in 1993 in El Paso, and proved an immediate success. Agents and technology were concentrated in specific areas, providing a "show of force" to potential illegal border crossers. The drastic reduction in apprehensions prompted the Border Patrol to undertake a full-scale effort in San Diego, Calif., which accounted for more than half of illegal entries. Operation Gatekeeper was implemented in 1994, and reduced illegal entries in San Diego by more than 75% over the next few years. A defined national strategic plan was introduced alongside Operation Gatekeeper and set out a plan of action for the Border Patrol into the future. With illegal entries at a more manageable level, the patrol was able to concentrate on other areas, such as establishing anti-smuggling units and search and rescue teams like BORSTAR. The Border Safety Initiative (BSI) was created in 1998 with a commitment by the Border Patrol and the promised cooperation of the Mexican government.

Homeland security became a primary concern of the nation after the Sept. 11 terrorist attacks. Border security became a topic of increased interest in Washington, D.C. Funding requests and enforcement proposals were reconsidered as lawmakers began reassessing how the nation's borders must be monitored and protected. On March 1, 2003, the Department of Homeland Security (DHS) was established, and the U.S. Border Patrol became part of U.S. Customs and Border Protection, a component of DHS.

The U.S. Border Patrol continues its efforts to control the nation's borders. The 21st century promises to provide enormous leaps in technology that can be applied to border enforcement. The modernization of the Border Patrol advances at a dizzying rate as new generations of agents develop innovative ways to integrate the contemporary technology into field operations. New and specialized technology is being created within the Border Patrol that holds increasing potential to assist agents in fulfilling the mission of the Border Patrol.

What is the public opinion of the Borderland toward border patrols?

In a survey done by the *Dallas Morning News*, 65% of U.S. border cities answered that they definitely do not need more security on their borders, nor a wall; 75% of Mexican cities answered they don't need more CBP security or a border barrier.[17]

What is "Hold the Line"?

Operation Hold the Line was a preventive measure taken by the U.S. Border Patrol, initiated on Sept. 19, 1993. Originally, the operation was named

17 http://interactives.dallasnews.com/2016/border-poll/

Operation Blockade. The location of the operation was on the U.S.-Mexico border between Ciudad Juárez and El Paso. Silvestre Reyes, who was the head of the El Paso Border Control at the time, ordered his officers to form a human and vehicle blockade along the border. Operation Hold the Line was the first operation of its kind and represented a shift in ideology in policing illegal immigration. Previous policies focused on finding and deporting illegal immigrants who had already crossed the border. Operation Hold the Line instead focused on intercepting and preventing illegal entries at the border. The operation immediately affected El Paso and the surrounding areas. Operation Hold the Line was credited with a 72% drop in apprehensions in the El Paso sector (covering the border area between Tucson, Ariz., and Marfa, Texas) between fiscal 1993 and 1994, when other sectors averaged only a 3% drop. It was also seen as the cause of 286,000 fewer illegal crossings in 1994, 146,000 fewer in 1996, and 105,000 fewer in the first nine months of 1997 in the El Paso sector.[18]

How many undocumented immigrants are stopped by border patrol? Which countries do they come from?

The Border Patrol in 2018 reported 310,531 apprehensions nationwide. More than 25,000 of

18 https://organpipehistory.com/orpi-a-z/
operation-hold-the-line-2/

those apprehensions were in El Paso. Another 180,000 were from countries other than Mexico.

Top Ten Largest U.S. Immigrant Groups, 2016[19][20]

Mexico	26.5%
India	5.6%
China	4.9%
Philippines	4.4%
El Salvador	3.2%
Vietnam	3.1%
Cuba	2.9%
Dominican Republic	2.5%
Korea	2.4%
Guatemala	2.1%

What is the SENTRI program?

The Secure Electronic Network for Travelers Rapid Inspection (SENTRI) is a U.S. Customs and Border Protection program that allows expedited clearance for pre-approved, low-risk travelers upon arrival in the U.S. Participants may enter the U.S by using dedicated primary lanes into the U.S at southern land border ports. Travelers must be pre-approved for the SENTRI program. All applicants undergo a rigorous background check and in-person interview before enrollment.

---

19 https://www.migrationpolicy.org/programs/data-hub/charts/largest-immigrant-groups-over-time
20 http://www.latimes.com/nation/la-na-border-apprehensions-20170309-story.html

What is a laser visa? How much does it cost?

The Border Crossing Card (BCC) is both a BCC and a B1/B2 visitor's visa. A BCC, also referred to as a DSP-150, is issued as a laminated card, which has enhanced graphics and technology, similar to the size of a credit card. It is valid for travel until the expiration date on the front of the card, usually 10 years after issuance.

Border Crossing Card Validity

- The new card is valid for 10 years after issuance, except in the cases of some children (see Border Crossing Card Fees).
- "Laser visas" issued prior to Oct. 1, 2008, are still valid for travel until the expiration date on the front of the card.

Qualifying for a Border Crossing Card

- B1/B2 visa/border crossing cards are only issued to applicants who are citizens of and resident in Mexico.
- Applicants must meet the eligibility standards for B1/B2 visas.
- They must demonstrate that they have ties to Mexico that would compel them to return after a temporary stay in the U.S.

Applying for a Border Crossing Card

BCC applicants must make an application using the normal procedures set by consular sections in Mexico.

Required Documentation

All applicants for a B1/B2 visa/border crossing card must have a valid Mexican passport at the time of application.

Border Crossing Fees[21]

Nonimmigrant visa application processing fee (non-refundable) for all categories:

Non-petition-based nonimmigrant visa (except E): $160.00

Includes (but not limited to), the following visa categories:

B   Visitor Visa: Business, Tourism, Medical Treatment

C-1   Transiting the United States

D   Crewmembers – Airline, Ship

F   Student, Academic

I   Media and Journalists

J   Exchange Visitors

        *Applicants for J visas participating in official U.S. government-sponsored educational and cultural exchanges: No fee (See Exchange Visitor Visas (https://travel.state.gov/content/travel/en/us-visas/study/exchange.html#govnofee) for further detailed fee information.)

M   Students, Vocational

TN/TD NAFTA Professionals

---

21 Fee amounts are from 2019: https://travel.state.gov/content/travel/en/us-visas/visa-information-resources/fees/fees-visa-services.html

T   Victim of Trafficking in Persons

U   Victim of Criminal Activity

Petition based visa categories: $190.00

Includes these visa categories:

H   Temporary Workers/Employment or Trainees

L   Intracompany Transferees

O   Persons with Extraordinary Ability

P   Athletes, Artists and Entertainers

Q   International Cultural Exchange

R   Religious Worker

- E - Treaty trader/investor, Australian professional specialty category visa: $205
- K - Fiancé(e) or spouse of U.S. citizen category visa: $265

Border Crossing Card Fees[22]

- Border crossing card - age 15 and over (valid 10 years): $160
- Border crossing card - under age 15; for Mexican citizens if parent or guardian has or is applying for a border crossing card (valid for 10 years or until the applicant reaches age 15): $16.00

Other Fees

- L visa fraud prevention and detection fee

---

22 Fee amounts are from 2019: https://travel.state.gov/content/travel/en/us-visas/tourism-visit/border-crossing-card.html

- for visa applicant included in L blanket petition (principal applicant only): $500
- The Consolidated Appropriations Act of 2016 (Public Law 114-113) increases fees for certain H-1B and L-1 petitioners. Consular sections collect this fee for blanket L-1 visa applications (principal applicant only) filed by petitioners who employ 50 or more individuals in the United States if more than 50% of those individuals are in H-1B or L-1 nonimmigrant status: $4,500

What is la Línea Express?

People along the border, mostly Ciudad Juárez residents, refer to the SENTRI program as "la Línea Express." SENTRI is a relatively new name.

What are the documentation fees?

USCIS is almost entirely funded by application and petition fees. The following are the different type of fees:

Immigration Benefit Request	Fee ($USD)
G–1041 Genealogy Index Search Request	$65
G–1041A Genealogy Records Request (Copy from Microfilm)	$65
G–1041A Genealogy Records Request (Copy from Textual Record)	$65
I–90 Application to Replace Permanent Resident Card	$455
I–102 Application for Replacement/Initial Nonimmigrant Arrival-Departure Document	$445
I–129/129CW Petition for a Nonimmigrant worker	$460
I–129F Petition for Alien Fiancé(e)	$535
I-130 Petition for Alien Relative	$535
I-131/I-131A Application for Travel Document	$575
I–140 Immigrant Petition for Alien Worker	$700
I–191 Application for Relief Under Former Section 212(c) of the Immigration and Nationality Act (INA)	$930
I–192 Application for Advance Permission to Enter as Nonimmigrant	$585/$930
I–193 Application for Waiver of Passport and/or Visa	$585
I–212 Application for Permission to Reapply for Admission into the U.S. After Deportation or Removal	$930
I–290B Notice of Appeal or Motion	$675
I–360 Petition for Amerasian Widow(er) or Special Immigrant	$435
I–485 Application to Register Permanent Residence or Adjust Status	$1,140
I–485 Application to Register Permanent Residence or Adjust Status (certain applicants under the age of 14 years)	$750
I–526 Immigrant Petition by Alien Entrepreneur	$3,675
I–539 Application to Extend/Change Nonimmigrant Status	$370
I–600/600A Petition to Classify Orphan as an Immediate Relative/Application for Advance Petition Processing of Orphan Petition	$775

Immigration Benefit Request	Fee ($USD)
I-601 Application for Waiver of Ground of Excludability	$930
I-601A Application for Provisional Unlawful Presence Waiver	$630
I-612 Application for Waiver of the Foreign Residence Requirement (Under Section 212(e) of the INA, as Amended)	$930
I-687 Application for Status as a Temporary Resident under Section 245A of the Immigration and Nationality Act	$1,130
I-690 Application for Waiver of Grounds of Inadmissibility	$715
I-694 Notice of Appeal of Decision	$890
I-698 Application to Adjust Status From Temporary to Permanent Resident (Under Section 245A of the INA)	$1,670
I-751 Petition to Remove Conditions on Residence	$595
I-765 Application for Employment Authorization	$410
I-800/800A Petition to Classify Convention Adoptee as an Immediate Relative/Application for Determination of Suitability to Adopt a Child from a Convention Country	$775
I-800A Supp. 3 Request for Action on Approved Form I-800A	$385
I-817 Application for Family Unity Benefits	$600
I-824 Application for Action on an Approved Application or Petition	$465
I-829 Petition by Entrepreneur to Remove Conditions	$3,750
I-910 Application for Civil Surgeon Designation	$785
I-924 Application for Regional Center Designation Under the Immigrant Investor Program	$17,795
I-924A Annual Certification of Regional Center	$3,035
I-929 Petition for Qualifying Family Member of a U-1 Nonimmigrant	$230
N-300 Application to File Declaration of Intention	$270

23

---

23 Fee amounts are from 2019: https://www.uscis.gov/forms/our-fees

Immigration Benefit Request	Fee ($USD)
N–336 Request for Hearing on a Decision in Naturalization Proceedings	$700
N–400 Application for Naturalization	$640
N–470 Application to Preserve Residence for Naturalization Purposes	$355
N–565 Application for Replacement Naturalization/ Citizenship Document	$555
N–600/N–600K Application for Certificate of Citizenship	$1,170
USCIS Immigrant Fee	$220
Biometric Services Fee	$85

What is dual citizenship?

The U.S. government does not formally recognize dual citizenship, and it can be a risk of losing U.S. citizenship. The government reasons that when a person becomes a citizen of a foreign country, the person is in allegiance with the foreign country. However the government has not sought out these citizens.

How many people cross the border?

In 2016, 42 million people crossed into the U.S. using 16 pedestrian bridges. Considering the estimates from the Migration Policy Institute indicating that the population of the border cities will double in the next 30 years, the number of legal crossings should rise.

Officers from the Ciudad Juarez Police Department's special Delta unit patrol outside its headquarters recently.

Officer Robert Romero, left, and Officer William Hooks patrol El Paso's northeast part of the city.

Border Crime

Cities on the U.S. side of the border are among the safest cities in America measured by virtually any statistic.

However, the border cities of El Paso, Texas, and San Ysidro, Calif., have suffered tragedies over the years. On Aug. 3, 2019, a man from Allen, Texas, killed 22 people at a Walmart in the seventh deadliest mass shooting in modern U.S. history. Another 24 people were injured. The assailant gave himself up to police.

In San Ysidro on July 18, 1984, a 41-year-old man fatally shot 21 people and wounded 19 others at a McDonald's restaurant. He was killed by a police sniper.

How is one of the safest cities in the U.S. next to one of the most dangerous cities in the world?

El Paso, with a population of nearly 700,000 in 2019, is said to be among the top ten safest cities in the U.S., according to several surveys. For example, violent crime for El Paso this year was 3.9 per 1,000 residents, compared to a national average of 4.49 per 1,000 persons; property crime for El Paso is 18.9 per 1,000 residents; the national average for property crimes is 27.11 per 1,000 residents.[24][25]

Excluding these mass shootings, border cities on the U.S. side are among the safest in the country. For example, a total of 21 homicides and 335 rapes were registered in 2014; 17 homicides and 322 rapes in 2015; and 17 homicides and 314 rapes in 2016. These crimes include robbery, assault, vehicle or personal property theft, rape and murder, according to the city of El Paso website. El Paso averages about 20 homicides per year, a small number for a city of its size.

Ciudad Juárez, Chihuahua, El Paso's sister city across the border, is a different story. With a population of nearly 1.5 million people, this city has been the site of violent cartel and drug-related crimes. Violence began to rise in this city in 2013, when the Carrillo-Fuentes cartel and the Beltran-Leyva cartel began fighting for control of the city. This led to a total of 438 deaths in 2014, 312 deaths in 2015 and 545 deaths in 2016. It is important to note that most of these victims were related to a gang or a cartel, and innocent bystanders were rarely injured in these attacks. Crimes in this city included kidnapping, extortion, robbery, money laundering, aggravated assault, rape and murder, according to the National Institute of Statistics and Geography in Mexico (INEGI) website. Unfortunately, murder rates in Ciudad Juárez have not decreased and continue to rise.

---

24 https://www.cityrating.com/crime-statistics/texas/el-paso. html
25 https://www.safewise.com/blog/safest-metro-cities/

Since Chihuahua's current governor, Javier Corral, was elected in early late 2016, more than 1,000 homicides have been committed in Ciudad Juárez. In 2018, a total of 39 murders were registered in January and 18 in February, for a total of 57 murders.

How safe is the rest of the U.S.-Mexico border?

According to data from the INEGI & CDC website, the violence rates on the rest of the U.S.-Mexico border are quite high as well. Comparing the violence index from Mexico and U.S. involving drug-and-crime-related incidents by state yields the following statistics:

- Baja California, Mexico recorded a total of 37,583 deaths in 2014, 30,786 in 2015 and 39,886 in 2016.

- Chihuahua, Mexico recorded a total of 22,395 deaths in 2014, 23,993 deaths in 2015 and 26,898 deaths in 2016.

- Sonora, Mexico recorded a total of 24,246 deaths in 2014, 29,587 deaths in 2015 and 33,268 deaths in 2016.

- Coahuila, Mexico recorded a total of 17,080 deaths in 2014, 21,501 deaths in 2015 and 18,893 deaths in 2016.

- Nuevo Leon, Mexico recorded a total of 24,250 deaths in 2014, 25,203 deaths in 2015 and 26,979 deaths in 2016.

- Tamaulipas, Mexico recorded a total of 23,339 deaths in 2014, 18,908 deaths in 2015 and 19,428 deaths in 2016.
- California, U.S.A. recorded a total of 4,748 deaths in 2014 and 5,082 deaths in 2015.
- Arizona, U.S.A. recorded a total of 1,239 deaths in 2014 and 1,334 deaths in 2015.
- New Mexico, U.S.A. recorded a total of 471 deaths in 2014 and 547 deaths in 2015.
- Texas, U.S.A. recorded a total of 4,212 deaths in 2014 and 4,741 deaths in 2015.

It is important to point out that the states of Chihuahua and Sonora presented the highest number of crimes against women. Data for the U.S. border states for 2016 was not available.

How are border cities categorized?

Border cities are under a contingency plan that was first established in 1983 by the Joint Response Team (JRT). A total of 28 cities are located along the border. Fourteen are located in the U.S. and 14 in Mexico. Under the Border 2012 Program, a 15th border city was acknowledged: the Tohono O'odham nation, located between the states of Arizona and Sonora, Mexico. Under the Border 2012 Program, El Paso, Texas and Ciudad Juárez, Chihuahua also included Sunland Park, New Mexico, and the Ysleta del Sur Pueblo to the sister city plan, generating a tri-national party.

The border cities are categorized into Region 9 and Region 6. Region 9 is composed of:

- San Diego, California - Tijuana, Baja California
- Calexico (Imperial county), California - Mexicali, Baja California
- Yuma-San Luis, Arizona - San Luis Rio Colorado, Sonora
- Nogales, Arizona - Nogales, Sonora
- Naco (Cochise county), Arizona - Naco, Sonora
- Douglas, Arizona - Agua Prieta, Sonora
- Tohono O'odham Nation, Arizona - Sonoyta, Sonora

The region 6 border cities are:

- Columbus, New Mexico - Puerto Palomas, Chihuahua
- El Paso, Texas - Ciudad Juárez, Chihuahua - Sunland Park, New Mexico - Ysleta del Sur Pueblo (Tri-National party)
- Presidio, Texas - Ojinaga, Chihuahua
- Del Rio, Texas - Ciudad Acuña, Coahuila
- Laredo, Texas - Nuevo Laredo, Tamaulipas
- McAllen, Texas - Reynosa, Tamaulipas
- Brownsville, Texas - Matamoros, Tamaulipas

Source: Environmental Protection Agency website.

What is the extent of drug violence on the Mexican side of the border compared to the U.S. side of the border?

Mexico has always been blamed for the amount of illegal narcotics introduced into the U.S. It is important to establish that drugs are very much present on both sides of the border.

Marijuana, methamphetamines, heroin and cocaine are four of the most common drugs confiscated on the U.S.-Mexico border, according to U.S. Customs and Border Patrol and the Texas Department of Public Safety.

The border patrol has confiscated the highest amount of drugs in the states of Arizona, California and Texas. According to data from the DEA website, there has been a 50% increase in drug overdose cases in the U.S. as of 2015.

In 2017, U.S. Customs and Border Patrol seized almost $1 million dollars worth of methamphetamines, cocaine and heroin coming in from Mexico in only three days.

Crystal methamphetamine consumption has increased greatly in the last five years. Crystal methamphetamine is a fairly new drug that sells for a low price because it is extremely easy and cheap to make, compared to the cost of other drugs like marijuana or cocaine.

Do the U.S. and Mexican governments work together in an effort to try to stop drugs, weapon and human trafficking across the border?

Teamwork between both countries has always been present near the border. Both countries enjoy good communication and alliance when working together to try to stop the drug and weapon trafficking occurring through the border.

"When we are investigating a criminal act of violence, especially one of big impact, there is a lot of communication between us and the American authorities in case this person flees the country," said Ramon Galindo Noriega, Mexico's sub-secretary for the state of Chihuahua.

Both governments also work together in the context of deportations. According to Noriega, the number of deportees has significantly decreased in the last 15 months. "We used to receive up to 35 deportees every day and now we only receive up to 15 deportees a day," Noriega said.

Are there cross-border gangs? How prevalent are they?

Gangs are active on both sides of the border. Some of them, coming from Mexico and South America, have spread at an alarming rate in the U.S.

Violence in the U.S. reached its peak during the mid-1980s due to an increase in gang-related crimes. Many of these gangs evolved from previous generations, while others have been created from scratch.

Some of the largest gangs on the U.S. side of the border are now beginning to represent an even bigger threat, since they have been dividing into branches and have started to fight for leadership. This has resulted in major acts of violence near the border in the past 10 years.

According to data retrieved from the National Gang Intelligence Center website, the state of California has the Mexican Mafia, MS-13 (Mara Salvatrucha), MS-18 (18th Street Gang) and the Sureños (Sur 13). Arizona has the Arizona Mexican Mafia, Barrio Azteca, MS-13, Sureños and Westside. New Mexico has Barrio Azteca, Latin Kings, MS-13 and New Mexico Syndicate. Texas has the most gangs with a total of 10. They are the Bandidos, Barrio Azteca, Hermanos de Pistoleros Latinos, Latin Kings, Sureños, Tango Blast, Tri-City Bombers, Texas Chicano Brotherhood, Texas Mexican Mafia (Mexikanemi) and Texas Syndicate.

Gangs are active on the border and continue to recruit members as young as 12 years old, introducing them to a risky life of kidnappings, murders and drug trafficking. This method is effective because these kids can not be charged and are released after a few hours of detainment.

Although these are the most prevalent gangs near the border, there are currently around 34,000 gangs in the U.S., with a total of approximately 1.3 million members, according to the National Gang Intelligence Center.

Which cartels pose the biggest threat to the U.S.-Mexico border?

Mexican cartels originated in the 1980s with the Guadalajara cartel, which introduced large-scale smuggling of marijuana and opium through the U.S.-Mexico border.

A few years later, several other Mexican cartels began to gain dominance, including the Tijuana cartel led by the Arellano Felix brothers, the Juárez cartel led by the Carrillo Fuentes family, the Sonora cartel led by Miguel Caro Quintero and the Zetas.

The Sinaloa cartel, led by Joaquin El Chapo Guzman, has become one of the most notorious cartels, along with its branch, the Beltran-Leyva cartel. Although these cartels are headquartered in Sinaloa, a Mexican state located far south of the border, they play a big role in crimes occurring at the border.

These cartels, along with the Juárez cartel, pose the biggest threat to the border, Galindo Noriega said. The never-ending drug war in the city of Juárez, Chihuahua, originated due to a conflict between these two cartels and the cartel of Guerrero, Mexico. The cartel of Guerrero wanted to participate in the drug smuggling across the border, but since the territory was already in a war between the Sinaloa and the Juárez cartel, tremendous bloodshed ensued.

Is violence against women prominent on the border?

Violence against women has always existed, especially in countries where men think of themselves as superior to women, commonly known as "machismo" in Spanish-speaking countries.

Violence against women on the U.S.-Mexico border appears to be very high. Some say that an increase in violence against women began in 1994, with the arrival of maquiladoras to the border cities. These factories employ thousands of women. According to the INEGI website, a total of 500 women have been brutally murdered in the border city of Juárez, Chihuahua and many more disappeared, leaving no trace of their whereabouts. Most of these crimes remain unsolved, given that influential people both in society and the government are allegedly involved, according to journalist Diana Washington Valdez, who wrote a book about these murders and also participated in the making of a documentary called *Border Echoes* after a seven-year investigation of the drug war.

"I felt this was my contribution to the knowledge base for these crimes," Washington Valdez said. Most of these women were working-class individuals who went missing on their way home after leaving their workplace or school. These murders are known as "feminicidios."

This particular region shows high numbers of violent crimes against women in contrast with other border cities, but this type of crime is even more prominent in the south of Mexico, especially in Mexico City and its surrounding areas, according to Galindo Noriega.

What are other prevalent crimes along the border?

Gun smuggling and human trafficking are also very prevalent in the U.S.-Mexico border region, according to U.S Immigration and Customs Enforcement (ICE). Regardless of the government's efforts to stop gun smuggling, the number of guns confiscated has not dropped. According to ICE, about 2,000 illegal weapons cross the border into U.S. territory on a daily basis. It is important to note that such weapons come from the U.S., moving into Mexico.

Firearms are relatively cheap to acquire in the U.S., especially cheap military and assault weapons. This is the main reason why these arms are smuggled into Mexico daily, leading to a massive business at the U.S.-Mexico border.

Another crime prevalent on the border is human trafficking. Traffickers illegally introduce people into the U.S. who are seeking a better life or who are victims of drug cartels and are trying to escape violence.

According to ICE, about 410,000 undocumented people attempting to enter the country illegally were caught in 2017, including more than 30,000 children. Most of these individuals come from Guatemala, El Salvador, Honduras and parts of Mexico.

How prominent is corruption on the border? Are there joint task forces fighting crime on the border?

In recent years, more than 140 Border Patrol agents have been arrested and charged with corruption, which represents 1% of the total number of active agents. Some of the charges include providing sensitive information to cartels and accepting bribes, which leads to the free movement of drugs and guns across the border.

According to the Department of Homeland Security, these corrupt agents pose a national threat. and the problem could intensify due to President Trump's executive order to hire 5,500 additional border patrol agents.

Since the arrival of the current governor of Chihuahua, Javier Corral Jurado, in October 2016, many politicians have been detained and prosecuted for corruption and misuse of power. One of the most renowned cases is the ongoing investigation of the former governor of Chihuahua Cesar Duarte who is wanted for electoral charges and corruption.

"We do not tolerate corruption coming from any individual in our governmental team," said Galindo Noriega. The Mexican government is constantly being monitored by the Mexican Ministry of Public

Administration in an effort to detect any corrupt activities from public officials.

How accurate are the movies and documentaries in portraying the truth about the drug war?

Many movies and documentaries have been made about the ongoing drug war at the border, portraying different perspectives on the drug war. Some do it by telling the story of victims who survived an attack, others by showing how drugs are smuggled across the border and some by portraying cartels and gangs fighting over territory.

Many of the moviemakers visit Ciudad Juárez, Mexico to do research about the subjects prior to making the movie.

Sicario, Border Echoes, Señorita Extraviada and *Bordertown* are some of the movies and documentaries about this border-city problem.

Two young men are draped in U.S. and Mexico flags as they head to the Hugs not Walls event in El Paso, Texas. Photo by Stella M. Chávez/KERA News.

Family members from El Paso and Ciudad Juarez greet at Hugs not Walls. Photo by Dino Chiecchi.

Border Art and Culture

What are telenovelas?

Telenovelas are television soap operas. Telenovelas originally grew out of radionovelas. Radionovelas consisted of small 15-minute segments that were mostly geared toward housewives. Telenovelas grew from the 15-minute segments to 30 minutes and then an hour long, with story lines written for middle class viewers in the 1950s. Telenovelas began to include overblown plots and overt sexual nudity. These plots included controversial and scandalous issues such as deception, incest, murder and adultery. One of the very first globally known telenovela was "Los Ricos También Lloran," or "The Rich Also Cry." It aired in Mexico in 1979 and was then exported to Russia, China and the U.S.[26]

When and where was the first Thanksgiving?

The first Thanksgiving was celebrated along the Rio Grande near San Elizario, Texas. Although many

26 https://www.britannica.com/art/telenovela

Americans celebrate the first Thanksgiving from the Pilgrims, the actual first Thanksgiving was celebrated in new El Paso. It took place on April 30, 1598, during Spanish explorer Juan de Oñate's expedition to unexplored land which is now part of New Mexico. Juan de Oñate was a conquistador who sent out search parties in search of treasure, and in the process treated Native Americans poorly. For doing so, Juan de Oñate was later exiled from the colony, fined and deprived of his titles.[27]

What kinds of music are prevalent in the Borderland?

There are various types of music that are popular in the Borderland. Among the special genres are "oldies" and Mexican music like Duranguense, which is fast-paced and includes a "cowboy style" attire, Tejano music and Latin pop. Some popular artists include the late Selena, Alacranes Musical and MC Magic. Selena was a Tejano singer, born on April 16, 1971, and died on March 31, 1995 in Corpus Christi, Texas, after being shot by Yolanda Saldivar, the president of her fan club. The iconic Selena had a large impact on the Borderland community and more than 20 years after her slaying is still an icon in the Latin community.

Another iconic form of music in the Borderlands is mariachi. Identified as "a type of traditional Mexican folk music, typically performed by a small group

27 https://texasalmanac.com/topics/history/timeline/first-thanksgiving

of strolling musicians dressed in native costume,"
mariachi often consists of violins, a large bass guitar,
trumpets and one or two singers. Mariachi music is
influenced by Spanish music. Mariachis are typically
seen playing at parties, quinceañeras, weddings and
throughout festivals.[28]

What is a corrido/narcocorrido?

They are ballads in a traditional Mexican style,
typically having lyrics that narrate a historical event.
Corridos usually depict a story. They are a narration
and often also include personal stories of those
that sing them. Narcocorridos are quite similar to
corridos in the sense of telling a story. However,
narcocorridos narrate those stories of drug cartels or
drug ballads.

What is la Santa Muerte?

La Santa Muerte, also known as the Holy Death, is
a female deity in Mexican Catholicism. In some
cases, she is the Saint of Death. Many who believe
in the Santa Muerte have prayed to her. She is also
worshipped by many drug cartels. La Santa Muerte
devotees continues to grow, boasting up to 12
million followers. While she is uplifted by many, the
Catholic Church perceives La Santa Muerte to be a
"celebration of devastation and of hell." But, many of
the rituals involved in worshipping La Santa Muerte
are similar to that of Catholic customs, such as
rosaries, candles and prayers.

28 https://en.wikipedia.org/wiki/Tejano_music

What are some pastimes of the border?

Pastimes of the border include cockfights and charreadas. A charreada is similar to an American rodeo. A charreada dates back to colonial times in the context of estates that mixed farming and ranching. This also involves charrerias, a Mexican sport that demonstrates roping skills and horsemanship. Cockfights include betting on roosters in a fight. Often, the winner picks top roosters from the opposing fighters. The rooster that dies may also be eaten by the owners so it does not go to waste.[29]

Loteria is also a significant pastime that is largely celebrated to this day. It is also referred to as "Mexican bingo." Loteria involves cards that depict an image. The announcer or person dealing the cards will call out, for example, "el nopal" (the cactus) to indicate the image on the card and players will fill their "tabla" (game board) with the corresponding image. The winner shouts "Loteria!" to win the game.[30]

What dances are popular in the Borderland?

Folklorico is a term for Mexican dances that develop stories about culture within the community. Within El Paso there are many high schools that teach

29 https://www.gdltours.com/charreria.html
30 http://www.teresavillegas.com/history-of-la-loteria/

folklorico as a class to represent the deep and rich culture that Mexico and the Borderland share. Folklorico dancers are both male and female, though mainly female. Males wear boots and black attire, with large sombreros (hats), that are similar to mariachi uniforms, while females wear large dresses that are held by both ends by the dancers' hands. They sway, or flow, both ends of the dress as they dance.[31]

Another dance that is prevalent in the border community is the Danza de Matachines. The dancers are dressed in ritual attire called bouffon, inspired by a carnavalesque dance troupe which emerged in Spain in the early 17th century, influenced by similar European traditions, such as the moresca.[32]

Why are murals so common along the Borderland?

There are a large number of murals in Borderland cities. Many are found in primarily Mexican American neighborhoods, often of lower income status. These murals may include various religious views, cultural and native depictions. Many of them depicted within the Borderland are politically driven. Some examples include murals in El Paso's Segundo Barrio and in the downtown area as well. These murals, such as the Sacred Heart Mural, depict pastimes of the border, and small actions or representations that El Paso has experienced.

31 http://historyoffolklorico.blogspot.com/2008/04/most-people-in-our-society-do-not.html
32 https://www.archsa.org/news/a-new-tradition-at-an-old-mission-matachines-and-mission-concepcion

University of Texas at El Paso graduate Aaron Jones is a star running back for the Green Bay Packers. Photo by El Paso Times.

Mexican pop star Juan Gabriel was one of Ciudad Juarez's most famous residents and one of the country's most beloved artists. He died Aug. 28, 2016 at age 66.

Influential People

Who is Marty Robbins?

The Borderlands story includes many famous and influential people. One of the most widely known people who helped bring this story to light was not even from the border. Marty Robbins, the country music artist, sang "down in the West Texas town of El Paso" in a song titled "El Paso," which sold millions of records and cemented Rosa's Cantina, love and loss along the Rio Grande in the American psyche.

Who was Juan de Oñate?

Juan de Oñate was born in Zacatecas, Mexico in about 1550. In 1595, he was sent by King Philip II of Spain to lead an expedition to the north of Mexico into today's state of New Mexico. He was sent to spread Roman Catholicism, but he was most interested in silver.

Upon his arrival, the Acoma people received Oñate and fellow explorers with open arms, offering goods. In a declaration of power, he took anything he wanted from the indigenous people, demanding silver and allegiance to the Spanish crown. The Acoma people refused to be forced into accepting the new religion or the arbitrary killing of their own people. They revolted and killed 13 Spaniards, which prompted Oñate to destroy their village. He and the explorers killed and raped 300 women and children. Just 200 of the 2,000 Native Americans survived the uprising, but were sentenced by Oñate to the amputation of one foot and 20 years of servitude.

Years later, Oñate was tried in Mexico City and convicted of a dozen charges. He was eventually exiled from Mexico City and lived the rest of his life in Spain.

An equestrian sculpture of Oñate by the late well-known artist John Sherrill Houser was erected near the airport in El Paso. The huge statue was placed outside the city center so it would not be vandalized by a public still angry about his legacy.

The sculpture was part of a larger project of 12 statues commissioned by the city, known as "The Twelve Travelers Memorial of the Southwest." Only three have been completed, including the statue of Oñate entitled, "The Equestrian." The other is a statue of Fray Garcia de San Francisco entitled, "Founder of the Pass on the North," located in downtown El Paso in the Pioneer Plaza at the corner of El Paso and San Francisco Streets. The third and most recent installation is of Susan Shelby Magoffin entitled, "Magoffin Family Santa Fe-Chihuahua Trail

Monument," which is located at Keystone Heritage Park.[33][34]

Who was Pancho Villa? Why is he considered a hero by the Mexican people? What was his connection to El Paso?

Pancho Villa, whose real name was Doroteo Arango, was a Mexican revolutionary leader who led a rebellion against the president of Mexico Porfirio Diaz. Diaz was the only president ever to have ruled for over 10 years, a period of corruption that ignited the Mexican Revolution.

Villa is considered a hero for Mexicans because he was the only one to defeat the American military that was sent into Mexico. Americans say they retreated due to the start of World War I.

He became leader of the Division del Norte cavalry and governor of Chihuahua. He was an advocate for education and built some 30 schools in the state of Chihuahua. He was responsible for the killing of more than 30 Americans. The killings drew the attention of the U.S. government, which sent its military to capture him. The hunt for Pancho Villa lasted 11 months but he was never captured. He lived a quiet life on his ranch just outside Hidalgo del Parral, Chihuahua, until his assassination there in 1923. The revolution ended when Villa won a

33 http://www.pbs.org/pov/lastconquistador/background/
34 http://xiitravelers.org/

decisive battle in Juaréz, which resulted in Diaz abdicating his rule ending his dictatorship.[35] [36]

Who is El Chapo Guzman?

Joaquin Guzman Loera, known as El Chapo, began transporting drugs in the 1970s and 1980s from La Sierra in Sinaloa, Mexico to other major cities in Mexico and U.S. In 1993, he fled from Mexico to Guatemala, where he was captured by the police and sentenced to 20 years in prison for murder and drug trafficking. On Jan. 19, 2001, he escaped from prison, which cost him $2.5 million, according to authorities. In February 2014, after being on the run for 13 years, he again was captured by police in Mazatlan, Sinaloa. In July 2015, he escaped from prison again through a tunnel in his cell shower. The tunnel was equipped with artificial light, air ducts and high quality construction material. He was then captured for the third time on Jan. 8, 2016 in Los Mochis, Sinaloa. He was extradited to the U.S. and was convicted in July 2019 of numerous crimes and is currently serving a life term in the maximum security Metropolitan Correctional Center in New York City, N.Y.[37] [38]

35 https://www.history.com/topics/pancho-villa
36 https://truewestmagazine.com/
pancho-villa-and-the-el-paso-connection/
37 https://www.rollingstone.com/culture/features/
el-chapo-the-life-and-crimes-of-a-drug-lord-20160111
38 https://www.cnn.com/2017/01/18/world/joaqun-el-chapo-
guzmn-fast-facts/index.html

Who is Ruben Salazar?

Born in Juárez and raised in El Paso, Ruben Salazar was a pioneering bilingual journalist who began his career at the former *El Paso Herald-Post* newspaper, and became a correspondent for the *Los Angeles Times* in 1959, where he covered various foreign assignments including the Vietnam War, the Cuban Revolution and the student revolt in Mexico City.

He became known for his hard-hitting columns on social justice issues and the plight of the Mexican American community. The book *Border Correspondent*, published after his death, is a collection of his stories and columns throughout his career. He left his position at the *Times* for a news job at KMEX Los Angeles to provide better and more accurate coverage of the Latino community. While covering the Chicano Moratorium anti-war protest in East Los Angeles on August 29, 1970, he was killed by a tear gas canister fired by a a law enforcement officer into a bar where protestors had gathered.

A U.S. stamp was issued in his honor, and a documentary on his life, *Man in the Middle*, was released on April 29, 2014.[39][40]

Who is Diana Washington Valdez?

As an investigative reporter at the *El Paso Times*, Diana Washington Valdez spent several years investigating the murders and disappearance of

---

39 https://www.ucpress.edu/book.php?isbn=9780520301061
40 http://www.pbs.org/program/ruben-salazar-man-middle/

women in neighboring Ciudad Juárez.

She retired from the *Times* in March 2016 and started her own multimedia company, Digie Zone Network. In 2006, she published *Harvest of Women*, a book about the killings that claimed many women's lives in Ciudad Juárez.

She has collaborated with different publications and documentaries, like *Border Echoes*, in A&E's *The Killing Season: Season 2*, and on the film *Sicario*.

She received the Latina Leader in Literature Award in Washington, D.C. Before her newspaper career, during her time in the military, she received the Meritorious Service Medal, Army Commendation Medal, Army Achievement Medal, the Cold War Recognition Certificate and others.[41][42][43]

Who is Khalid and what is his connection to the border?

The 19-year-old songwriter and singer prodigy moved to El Paso when he was in high school because of his mother, Sgt. 1st Class Linda Wolfe. He is now recognized worldwide and is touring with pop singer Lorde. He often performs in El Paso and other border communities.[44][45]

41 https://www.goodreads.com/book/show/802678.
The_Killing_Fields
42 https://www.npr.org/templates/story/story.
php?storyId=1532607
43 https://dianawashingtonvaldez.blogspot.mx/2018/01/diana-washington-valdez-diana.html
44 http://www.khalidofficial.com/
45 https://www.rollingstone.com/music/features/khalid-american-teen-is-freshest-surprising-debut-album-w494814

Who is Reies López Tijerina?

Reies López Tijerina was born on Sept. 21, 1926, in Fall City, Texas, and died on Jan. 19, 2015 in El Paso, Texas. He was a civil rights activist on behalf of various Latino issues and led a movement in the Southwest demanding the repatriation of land in New Mexico confiscated by Anglo surveyors in violation of the 1848 Treaty of Guadalupe Hidalgo in northern New Mexico from 1956 to 1976.

He was fought against discrimination, demanding first-class citizenship for the undocumented, economic opportunity, the right to speak Spanish and preserve the Chicano culture.[46]

Who is Marcelino Serna?

A citizen of Mexico who lived in El Paso, Texas, Serna volunteered for the U.S. Army during World War I. When this was discovered, he was given the option to withdraw but he chose to stay and continue fighting. Serna was honored with two Purple Hearts and the Distinguished Service Cross in 1918. He became the most decorated World War I veteran from Texas. After the war, he moved to Texas and obtained his citizenship in 1924.[47][48]

---

46 https://www.britannica.com/biography/
Reies-Lopez-Tijerina
47 https://hurd.house.gov/media-center/editorials/
uncommon-valor-story-marcelino-serna
48 https://newspaperarchive.com/
el-paso-herald-post-may-16-1942-p-40/

Who is Tom Lea and his father?

Tom Lea was a muralist, illustrator, war correspondent, portraitist, landscapist, novelist and historian. His murals date to the 1930s and are found in several cities across the country, including Washington, D.C., and El Paso, Texas.

He wrote and illustrated bestselling novels such as *The Brave Bulls* and *The Wonderful Country*. In his artwork, he illustrated exotic places like Ecuador and China, but most of his work concentrated around his home near the border between Mexico and the U.S.

Tom Lea's father, Thomas Calloway Lea Jr., was the mayor of El Paso, Texas, during the time of the Mexican Revolution from 1910 to 1920.[49][50]

Who is Gaspar Enriquez?

Gaspar Enriquez was born in 1942 and raised in El Paso, Texas in a low-income, immigrant neighborhood near the border with Ciudad Juárez called Segundo Barrio.

He is a Chicano artist and focuses on acrylic, airbrush portraits of people that interest him. His work has been sold to different museums, including the Tucson Museum of Art, El Paso Museum of Art, Lyndon Baines Johnson Library and the Albuquerque Museum of Art.

---

49 http://www.humanitiestexas.org/programs/tx-originals/list/tom-lea
50 https://tomlea.com/the-artist/biography/

His art was part of the Chicano Art/Resistance and Affirmation exhibit, which toured the U.S. from 1990 to 1993. This exhibit marked the first time that Chicano art was acknowledged by the press and important museums in the U.S.

He is now restoring an ancient adobe building at San Elizario, in El Paso's Mission Valley.[51]

Who is Salvador Belcorta?

Originally from El Paso, Texas, Salvador Belcorta is an activist for public health and education. He co-founded the Centro de Salud Familiar La Fe, located in Segundo Barrio, and throughout El Paso.

When he was 14 years old, Belcorta began volunteering at La Fe clinic and has been involved in it since then. He obtained his Bachelor of Arts degree in social work at The University of Texas at El Paso, and then a master's degree through a UT-Austin program in El Paso. He was head of Community Health Services at El Paso City-County Health District in 1992. He then became the CEO of La Fe. At that time, the budget of the program $3 million and there were about 70 employees. La Fe's budget is now about $27 million and employs 450 people.

He also created the Child and Adolescent Wellness Center, which helps people in need in El Paso. The Wellness Center deals with health issues, culture and technology for young people.[52] [53]

51 http://gasparenriquez.com/bio.php#start
52 https://lafe-ep.org/our-history/
53 http://www.elpasoinc.com/news/q_and_a/ salvador-balcorta-ceo-centro-de-salud-familiar-la-fe/

Who is Silvestre Reyes?

Silvestre Reyes was born in Canutillo, Texas, and grew up on a farm in El Paso. The oldest of 10 children, he didn't learn to speak English until he was 6 years old. Reyes served in the U.S. Army during the Vietnam War from 1966 to 1968.

He later worked as a border patrol agent, immigration inspector and instructor at the Border Patrol Academy. He was promoted to sector chief in 1985 of the U.S. Border Patrol and managed operations both in McAllen and El Paso from 1984 to 1995. In 1996, he ran for the U.S. House of Representatives for the 16th District of Texas and won. He was defeated in 2012 by Robert "Beto" O'Rourke.

He is best known for implementing a border enforcement operation called Operation Hold the Line in 1993. A similar operation named Gatekeeper was implemented on the Tijuana border.

Operation Hold the Line resulted in the decline of immigrant entries to the U.S. but also increased the deaths of immigrants in more distant dangerous places.[54] [55]

article_cb046410-9241-11e1-bda8-001a4bcf6878.html
54 https://www.washingtonpost.com/blogs/the-fix/post/rep-silvestre-reyes-d-tex-defeated-by-beto-orourke/2012/05/30/gJQAM6cS1U_blog.html
55 https://www.texastribune.org/directory/silvestre-reyes/

Who is Veronica Escobar? What is her connection to El Paso?

A third generation El Pasoan, Democrat Veronica Escobar is one of two Latina women from Texas to be elected to the U.S. House of Representatives.

Her political career began through her nonprofit work as a communications director for former mayor, Raymond Caballero. After Caballero's failed reelection, Escobar was appointed county commissioner in 2006 and county judge in 2010.

Escobar resigned from her position in 2017 to run for Congress because of concern that the decisions made by the Trump Administration were hurting her hometown. She won the seat to represent Texas' 16th Congressional District.[56 57 58 59]

Who is Diana Natalicio? What is her connection to El Paso?

Diana Natalicio was born Diana Siedhoff on Aug. 25, 1939 in St. Louis, Mo. She studied Spanish as an undergraduate at Saint Louis University, completed her master's in Portuguese and earned her doctorate in linguistics while at the University of Texas at Austin.

56 https://escobar.house.gov
57 https://ballotpedia.org/Veronica_Escobar
58 https://www.elpasotimes.com/story/news/politics/elections/2018/03/09/veronica-escobar-election-history-first-texas-latina-us-congress/404466002/
59 https://www.texastribune.org/2017/08/25/el-paso-county-judge-veronica-escobar-announce-congressional-campaign/

She was hired as an academic administrator and became an assistant professor in 1971. Natalicio then served as vice president for academic affairs, dean of liberal arts, chair of the modern languages department and as a professor of linguistics. She was later named the contributing president at the University of Texas at El Paso in 1988, becoming the first woman to have the title. Natalicio retired from UTEP in August 2019 after serving 30 years as president, longer than any other sitting president at a U.S. major public doctoral and research university. She is also the longest serving woman president at a four-year public university. She has devoted much of her career to facilitating opportunities for students to engage and excel in their chosen fields of study, and is quick to recognize that students' talents are not limited based on where they are from nor their economic status.

She was named in *Time* magazine's Top 100 Most Influential People for all her works, effort, and major accomplishments for the University of Texas at El Paso and its students. Over 80% of UTEP's more than 23,000 students are Mexican American, and an additional 5% come from El Paso's sister city, Ciudad Juárez, Mexico. Enrollment grew to 25,000 students during her tenure, from 15,000 when she was appointed; UTEP became a major research institution, increasing research dollars from $6 million to more than $90 million annually; and doctoral programs grew from one to 22 during the same period.[60]

60 https://thecitymagazineelp.com/utep-president-dr-diana-natalicio-education-innovator-champions-access-excellence/

Who is Raymond L. Telles, Jr.?

Raymond Telles, born Sept. 5, 1915, was the first Mexican American mayor of a major American city, El Paso, Texas. He was also the first Hispanic appointed as a U.S. ambassador.

Born in El Paso and educated as an accountant, Telles worked at the U.S. Department of Justice for eight years. He was drafted into the Army in 1941. Telles then served in the U.S. Army Air Force, where he became chief of the Lend-Lease Program for Central and South America. Telles left the service with the rank of major.

Telles received the Peruvian Flying Cross, the Order of the Southern Cross from Brazil and the Mexican Legion of Merit and Colombian wings in recognition of the Lend-Lease Program. Telles served as aide to several Latin American and Mexican presidents visiting the U.S., and as military aide to Presidents Harry S. Truman and Dwight D. Eisenhower when they visited Mexico City.

Telles was elected county clerk for El Paso County, Texas in 1948. In 1951, Telles was recalled for the Korean War. He served as executive officer of the 67th Tactical and Reconnaissance Group, U.S. Air Force.

Telles was elected in 1957 mayor of El Paso and ran unopposed for a second term (1959-1961). He was appointed by President John F. Kennedy as ambassador to Costa Rica. In 1967, President Lyndon B. Johnson appointed Telles chairman of the U.S.-Mexican Border Commission.

In 1971, President Richard Nixon appointed him chairman of the Equal Employment Opportunity Commission for the U.S. Telles died on March 8, 2013 in Sherman Oaks, Calif., at the age of 97.[61]

Who is Pat Mora?

Poet Pat Mora was born in El Paso, Texas, and is a former teacher, university administrator, museum director and consultant. She is a popular national speaker who promotes creativity, inclusivity and bookjoy. She is the author of many books of poetry and children's books. *House of Houses*, published in 2008, is a family memoir told in the voices of ancestors. Her newest book of nonfiction is *Zing! Seven Creativity Practices for Educators and Students* (2010), according to the Poetry Foundation.

She has honorary doctorates from North Carolina State University and SUNY Buffalo, an honorary membership in the American Library Association, a Civitella Ranieri Fellowship to write in Umbria, Italy, and a Distinguished Alumni Award from the University of Texas at El Paso. She was a recipient and judge of a poetry fellowship from the National Endowment for the Arts and a recipient and advisor of the Kellogg National Leadership Fellowships. Mora and her husband live in Santa Fe, N.M., according to the Poetry Foundation's website.

61 https://archive.is/20130411053714/http://www.kvia.com/news/Former-Mayor-Raymond-L-Telles-Sr-has-died/-/391068/19244404/-/bmdbbl/-/index.html

Who is Vikki Carr?

Vikki Carr, born Florencia Bisenta de Casillas-Martinez Cardona to parents of Mexican ancestry on July 19, 1941, in El Paso, Texas, is an American vocalist who has had a singing career for more than four decades. She has performed in a variety of genres, but achieved the most success singing in Spanish. She established the Vikki Carr Scholarship Foundation in 1971. Carr achieved the most success in the 1960s and had 10 singles on the U.S. pop charts and 13 albums that made the U.S. non-album charts. She has been nominated for three Grammy Awards. Carr lives in San Antonio.

Who is Juan Gabriel?

Born Alberto Aguilera Valadez on Jan. 7, 1950, Juan Gabriel was a Mexican singer, songwriter and actor, also called Juanga and El Divo de Juárez. He was known for his flamboyant style, which broke barriers in the Latin music market. Widely considered one of the best and most prolific Mexican composers and singers of all time, he has been called a pop icon and sold more than 200 million records. Gabriel was among Latin America's best-selling singer-songwriters. Gabriel wrote some 1,800 songs, including one of the most popular Spanish-language songs of all time, "Amor Eterno." He also wrote "Querida," "Yo no nací para amar," "Hasta que te conocí," (https://en.wikipedia.org/wiki/Hasta_Que_Te_Conoc%C3%AD) and many others.

Gabriel fathered six children and never married. The mother of four of his children is Laura Salas. Gabriel died from a heart attack on Aug. 28, 2016. His body was cremated and his ashes were returned to the house he owned in Ciudad Juárez.

El Paso's bridges are among the busiest of the U.S.-Mexico border and account for billions of dollars of trade annually. Photo by El Paso Times.

Business

How many trucks cross from Mexico to the U.S. annually?

More than 5 million trucks cross from Mexico to the U.S. every year, according to the U.S. Department of Transportation. Laredo, Texas, is the top truck-crossing location with more than 2 million trucks crossing annually. California is next, with more than 800,000 truck crossings, followed by El Paso, Texas, with nearly 800,000.

Mexican border cities have a large manufacturing presence because of lower costs and proximity to many large U.S. cities. Among the businesses manufacturing in Mexico are companies in aerospace, automotive, electronics, home appliances and medical device industries. About 70% of Mexico's exports are destined for the U.S.

What is the USMCA?

The U.S.-Mexico-Canada Agreement replaced NAFTA, the North American Free Trade Agreement. The USMCA includes changes for automakers, stricter labor and environmental standards and other provisions.

USMC changes to NAFTA include:[62]

- Autos now must have 75% of their components manufactured in Mexico, the U.S. or Canada to quality for zero tariffs, according to Vox.com.
- Up to 45% of the parts must be made by workers who earn at least $16 an hour.
- Canada will grant more access to its dairy market to U.S. farmers.

What was NAFTA?

The North American Free Trade Agreement was an agreement that was signed by Canada, Mexico and the U.S. The agreement created a trilateral trade bloc in North America that allowed for free trade to occur between the three nations. It was signed in 1992 and went into effect on Jan. 1, 1994. It lifted tariffs on goods produced by the signatory countries, as well as "eliminated a 15-year barrier of cross-border investment, assisting in the trade movement of goods and services between the three countries."

How many commuter trucks and cars cross the border each day?

Data from 2009 to 2013 shows that commuter traffic from the U.S. side of the border to Mexico ranges from 10 million to 22 million personal vehicle commuters along the border each year. The number

62 https://ustr.gov/trade-agreements/free-trade-agreements/united-states-mexico-canada-agreement

of U.S. citizens who go to work in Mexico each day ranges anywhere from 105 crossings in Las Cruces, N.M., to 3,750 crossings at the El Paso, Texas port of entry. The number of people crossing the border varies in Arizona, California and Texas. In a survey taken in 2015, there were over 6 million pedestrian crossings and about 750,000 truck crossings. That same data reported that around 12 million personal vehicles crossed over with 20 million passengers and some 1,500 trains crossed that same year. These numbers have grown by a couple of thousand each year.

What is the local currency across the U.S.-Mexico border?

The local currency on the U.S. side of the border is the dollar. The currency used in Mexico is the peso. Depending on location and circumstance, both currencies are usually accepted on both sides of the border. For example, businesses closer to the international bridges and crossing areas are more likely to accept both the peso and the dollar. The exchange rate for the dollar to peso is currently at 19.28 pesos to one dollar, up from 18.44 in 2018.

This rate, though not the highest, was 21.89 in 2017, yet is much higher than the rate in 2013, which sank to 11.80. Trade, inflation, stock market movements and capital movements can all contribute to fluctuations.[63]

63 https://ycharts.com/indicators/
mexican_peso_exchange_rate

What is the economic impact of delayed border crossings?

Long wait times have the tendency to affect regional economies located near ports of entry. One of the impacts caused by delayed crossings is reduced cross-border shopping. According to a survey conducted at shopping areas of El Paso's Lower Rio Grande Valley, 57% of respondents said if they had to wait an hour to cross the bridge it would hinder their motivation to shop on the U.S. side. Not only do delayed crossings have an effect on local consumerism, they can also deter Mexican citizens from crossing the border to enjoy border-city entertainment in the U.S. In addition to the economic impact of delayed crossings, they also result in work and school tardiness for border commuters and cause a loss of business opportunities for local business owners interested in international trade.[64]

What is bottlenecking?

The term bottlenecking refers to congestion at ports of entry. Congestion at the border costs the U.S. $5.8 billion annually according to a report done by Accenture in 2008. That same year, 26,000 jobs and $1.4 billion in wages were lost, according to the same report. Bottlenecking is extremely costly and it is expected to skyrocket in coming years. One proposed solution involves staffing more customs

64 https://digitalcommons.utep.edu/cgi/viewcontent.cgi?article=1046&context=border_region

officials at ports of entry, which would allow more gates to be opened for commuters. More gates allow an easier flow of traffic, which can also be beneficial for importing and exporting products and goods. The ability to import and export goods efficiently offers the potential for an increase in regional economic growth.

The cost of cross-border transportation went up after the Sept. 11 terror attacks resulted in increased security. An increase in the number of Mexican trucks entering the U.S. ports of entry has also raised the cost of doing business at the border.[65]

What are tariffs and how do they affect the border economy?

A tariff, also known as a trade barrier or duty, is a tax on imports. Tariffs are usually charged at a fixed rate or as a percentage of the value of the goods. The main purpose for enacting tariffs on products and goods is to protect domestic industries from foreign competition, which helps raise revenue. Tariffs raise the prices on exported goods, which makes it difficult to compete in the trade market. The cost of production of domestic goods can increase as a result of taxed imports. This typically occurs when raw imported materials are needed for production. Furthermore, tariffs affect border economies by raising the price of goods, which results in a limited quantity. Limiting the amount of goods that are

65 https://digitalcommons.utep.edu/cgi/viewcontent. cgi?article=1046&context=border_region

imported also results in lower incomes, reduced employment and diminished economic output.[66][67]

66 https://www.investors.com/news/economy/what-is-a-tariff/
67 https://taxfoundation.org/impact-trade-tariffs-united-states/

El Pasoans built a makeshift memorial at the site of a Walmart where 22 people lost their lives and 24 more were injured Aug. 3 in a mass shooting. A Dallas-area man has been charged with the crime. Photo by El Paso Times.

Deaths

How many civilians have died as a result of Border Patrol encounters?

Migrants face a variety of dangers in their attempts to cross the U.S. border. Some of these dangers include dehydration, physical and sexual assault and abuse. Unfortunately, migrants also experience abuse, and in some cases, death, at the hands of Border Patrol agents. Since 2010, the Southern Border Communities Coalition recorded at least 83 deaths that have occurred as a result of Border Patrol and migrant encounters. These deaths, while tragic, involve multiple occurrences in which abuse was not a factor. Some of the deaths were a result of illness or circumstantial accidents that the parties involved had no control over.

These deaths have remained relatively low for the past nine years since the data was last recorded by the SBCC. At a time when border tensions remain high, and more migrants attempt to cross the border, federal agents may potentially resort to more violent and aggressive means of apprehending migrants.[68]

---

68 https://www.southernborder.org/deaths_by_border_patrol

What is femicide?

From 1993 to approximately 2005, more than 370 women and girls were killed in Ciudad Juárez. Many were the victims of torture prior to their violent deaths. The term femicide, or feminicidio in Spanish, became common as people became alarmed in border towns that the deaths were seemingly not investigated. A government committee found that half of the deaths were the result of motives like robbery and gang wars, while about 30% involved sexual assault.

The slayings received international attention, but little action took place on the part of the Mexican government to solve the murders. Evidence suggests some of the victims shared common characteristics, as did the crimes committed against them. Most of the victims were working at the city's factories, called maquiladoras, and some were students.

According to the World Health Organization, femicide is defined as the intentional killing of women because of their gender. Femicide committed by a spouse or lover is also recognized as intimate partner homicide or intimate femicide. Typically, femicide is associated with toxic masculinity, which devalues a woman's humanity. Mexico is notorious for crimes committed against women. Mexico ranks 16th in the world in homicides of women. Mexico's acknowledgement of the femicide epidemic after years of inaction has lead to the rise of counter-advocacy groups in the country. Mexico's failure to implement comprehensive measures that guarantee women a right to life results in tragedy as the murder rate of women in the country increases. Statistics gathered by the United Nations shows that 64,000 women and girls are killed annually. Other statistics show that femicide increased 500% from 2001-2010 in Mexico. Organizations like Nuestras Hijas Regeresan a Casa and Las Hijas De Violencia both attempt to combat what their government has failed to act upon. They unite in hope of bringing more attention to the issue by fighting for a right to life. Mexico's overt dismissal of the issue has led to protests by women in the country. A movement called Ni una mas ni una menos, which translates to "Not one more not one less" calls for justice for the women of Mexico. Terrified women in Mexico are now acting courageously by taking part in the dialogue.[69][70][71]

What are death rates among the detained?

Immigration detention centers have faced intense scrutiny because of their handling of detained migrants. These facilities have been monitored by the U.S. Department of Homeland Security. Their findings from 2003 to 2015 indicated that 144 migrant deaths during these years were due to uncontrollable circumstances. The variety of deaths

69 https://justiceinmexico.org/femicidesinmexico/
70 https://www.globalcitizen.org/en/content/
ni-una-mas-the-mexican-epidemic-of-femicide/
71 https://apps.who.int/iris/bitstream/handle/10665/77421/
WHO_RHR_12.38_eng.pdf

experienced in detention facilities are attributed to a multitude of variables. Some of these variables include illnesses such as cancer and liver disease. Other causes of death include infections, poor cardiovascular health and suicide. Since 2004, there has been a significant decline in the number of deaths occuring in detention facilities. In 2004, 32 deaths were recorded. The next decade saw a decrease in the number of deaths per year from 16 to 1.5, according to the U.S Department of Homeland Security. When categorized, cardiovascular deaths accounted for 33%, followed by cancer, which accounts for 16% of the deaths experienced in detention facilities. The Trump administration has put in place policies that makes it harder for illegal immigrants to get processed. In late 2018 and early 2019 the U.S. observed the arrival of immigrants trying to cross the American border in a caravan. This caravan brought with it people from Guatemala and Mexico. During the asylum process many migrants were detained in ICE facilities where the drastic increase in apprehensions has lead to another spike in mortality rates.[72][73][74]

How many migrants die every year crossing the border?

Border Angels, an organization dedicated to migrant rights, reform and the prevention of death have

72 https://www.bbc.com/news/world-latin-america-45951782
73 https://www.texastribune.org/2018/12/26/migrant-boy-death-el-paso-new-mexico-border/
74 https://www.ncbi.nlm.nih.gov/pmc/articles/PMC4661656/

recorded an estimated 10,000 deaths along the U.S.-Mexico border since 1994. The U.S. Customs Border and Protection has recorded 6,915 deaths in the years between 1998 and 2017. From 1995 to 2005, deaths doubled. From 2008 to 2017, the rate at which deaths occured decreased. The deaths that did occur are attributed to starvation, dehydration and heat stroke. Other causes include abuse by smugglers and attacks from desert wildlife. Migrants who cross the border by foot endure harsh conditions. Many migrants fail in their attempts to cross. This is linked to the disappearance of women and children. Advocacy groups like Border Angels, Humane Borders and Desert Angels, among many more, all work in conjunction to help assist struggling migrants. The type of aid provided by these organizations ranges from providing water to migrants on familiar crossing routes, to handling legal human rights cases and helping recover lost bodies of migrants. These organizations are nonprofits with a humanitarian obligation to help provide aid to those seeking asylum or an opportunity to better their lives.[75][76][77][78]

75 https://www.nnirr.org/drupal/border-groups
76 https://humaneborders.org/
77 https://losangelesdeldesierto.org/
78 https://www.nnirr.org/drupal/stopping-migrant-deaths

A private group called "We Build the Wall" on land owned by American Eagle Brick Company constructed a $6 million bollard-type wall at the border on private property near Mount Cristo Rey near land that separates New Mexico, Texas and the Mexican state of Chihuahua. Photo by Dino Chiecchi.

A fence separates El Paso and Ciudad Juarez on El Paso's West Side along Paisano Drive near the University of Texas at El Paso. The Rio Grande is on the other side of the fence acting as an additional, but natural boundary. Photo by Dino Chiecchi.

The Wall

What is the "wall"?

The U.S.-Mexico wall is a fence that measures up to 10 feet tall in some areas. It is a barrier meant to divide the two countries in order to limit and control movement through ports of entry. The wall is made of a series of walls and fences. The border's length is 1,989 miles (3,201 km). The southwest border runs between the U.S. and Mexico for nearly 2,000 miles. According to U.S. Customs and Border Protection, the wall only covers about 654 miles of the border.[79] [80]

Was the fence built all in one go?

No. There were three operations put in place in order to complete the building of the wall. Operation Hold the Line in Texas in 1993, Operation Gatekeeper in California in 1994, and Operation Safeguard in Arizona in 1994. These particular sites were chosen for the initial building of the wall because of the belief that illegal crossings were high in these areas. The U.S.-Mexico border wall is located along stretches of California/Baja California, Arizona/Sonora, New Mexico/Chihuahua and Texas and several Mexican states.

79 https://www.cbp.gov/border-security/ports-entry
80 https://fas.org/sgp/crs/homesec/R43975.pdf

Are there parts of the border without a barrier?

Yes. There is a wall and/or fence along 700 miles of the border on federal property and wherever there is not a natural barrier, such as the Rio Grande. In areas where the terrain makes it extremely difficult to cross the border on foot, short fences prevent vehicle access.

What does the wall symbolize for residents of the U.S. and Mexico?

It symbolizes economic, political and social division between the two neighboring countries. It also symbolizes the economic and social separation between the U.S. and Mexico.

Follow this link: http://interactives.dallasnews.com/2016/border-poll/ to view the results of a border survey conducted by Cronkite News at Arizona State University, Univision and the Dallas Morning News. The survey uses data from 14 different cities, seven on each side of the border. It answers questions such as "Should the U.S. build a wall to secure the border between Mexico and the U.S.?" and "What are the biggest problems you and your family currently face?"

How much money has the U.S. spent to build the wall that already exists?

The average mile of border wall costs taxpayers $4.5 million. In some places, the cost of construction has exceeded $12 million per mile. As of April 2009, $43.1 billion had been allocated by Congress for border wall construction and $2.4 billion had been spent. According to the U.S. Army Corps, maintenance of the border wall in some areas could cost $5 million to $9 million per mile per year.

What would it cost to build the wall that President Trump desires?

It is estimated that the proposed wall can potentially cost nearly $21.6 billion, not including maintenance.[81] The plan is to seal the border in three phases of construction of fences and walls covering just over 1,250 miles (2,000 km) by the end of 2020.

How does the current border barrier impact families that live on both sides?

The border barrier impacts people who live near it both physically and psychologically, as it takes a toll on their daily lives.[82] Thousands of people cross back and forth regularly to work and study, splitting

---

81 https://www.bbc.com/news/world-us-canada-37243269
82 http://bit.ly/2wRn5ip

their time between the two countries, while others do not even have the necessary documents to do so. Long waiting periods at the ports of entry, separation of families and, more recently, the fear of a border shutdown are some of the worries that are constantly in the back of people's minds. According to Bureau of Transportation Statistics provided by the U.S. Department of Transportation, there were more than 75,000,000 personal vehicles that crossed the border in 2018, with a daily average of approximately 200,000 vehicles that get in line to cross the border. Including the passengers in these vehicles, nearly 200,000,000 people crossed the border in 2018.

Follow this link to view Hunt Institute interactive commuter data: http://huntinstitute.utep.edu/data-indicators-for-the-region/interactive-data-tools/u-s-mexico-border-commuting-flows-u-s-residents-working-in-mexico-2009-2013

Consider the additional time and resources a person who commutes back and forth across the border will need to dedicate to be on time for work or school.

How tall is the current wall compared to the proposed wall?

The current border wall is 21 feet (6.4 meters) tall and 6 feet (1.8 meters) deep in the ground at its highest point. Other areas of the wall consist of 10-foot fences, or nothing at all. The wall that President Trump is proposing to build is currently being tested with eight different prototypes, ranging from 18 to 30 feet high. It also estimated to cost $18 billion. Four of the prototypes are concrete walls and four are made of other materials, including steel. Two prototypes have a "see through" component.[83][84]

Number of U.S.-Mexico b

Ports of Entry	Bus Passengers	Buses	Pedestrians
Douglas, AZ	25,339	2,501	847,56
Lukeville, AZ	2,874	532	46,49
Naco, AZ	675	22	152,16
Nogales, AZ	194,827	9,569	3,422,8
San Luis, AZ	169	169	2,640,90
Sasabe, AZ			52
Andrade, CA			901,6
Calexico East, CA	104,080	2,602	300,46
Calexico, CA			4,014,5
Cross Border Xpress, CA			1,279,0
Otay Mesa, CA	42,389	29,533	3,391,3
San Ysidro, CA	53,634	32,058	9,435,6
Tecate, CA			837,6
Columbus, NM	17,090	1,261	278,1
Santa Teresa, NM	2,270	232	145,7
Boquillas, TX			11,4
Brownsville, TX	46,609	6,239	2,893,4
Del Rio, TX			166,0
Eagle Pass, TX	62,010	2,688	703,6
El Paso, TX	195,808	15,977	7,218,4
Hidalgo, TX	263,682	20,026	2,170,3
Laredo, TX	816,696	38,996	3,701,1
Presidio, TX	2,071	1,246	252,0
Progreso, TX			1,034,1
Rio Grande City, TX			61,2
Roma, TX	7,909	401	229,2
Tornillo-Fabens, TX			37,9
Total	1,838,132	164,052	46,173,8

Source: U.S Department of Transportation: Bureau of Transportation Statistics

83 https://www.reuters.com/article/us-usa-trump-immigration-wall-exclusive-idUSKBN15O2ZN
84 https://www.reuters.com/article/us-usa-trump-immigration/trump-moves-ahead-with-wall-puts-stamp-on-u-s-immigration-security-policy-idUSKBN1591HP

er crossings in 2018

rsonal Vehicle Passengers	Personal Vehicles	Trucks
3,098,512	1,727,192	27,804
1,061,111	411,228	298
565,907	310,106	2,997
7,153,600	3,603,601	337,179
5,854,901	3,257,990	28,211
47,119	24,533	
1,118,965	575,493	
6,505,560	3,560,187	376,079
8,399,017	4,557,881	
13,318,027	7,708,214	962,577
25,182,134	14,505,306	
2,130,145	1,092,092	61,778
826,452	351,723	14,502
1,175,504	528,894	114,988
10,043,076	4,742,355	255,169
3,177,659	1,624,201	78,328
5,893,825	2,798,712	173,105
22,225,563	12,383,403	810,935
9,126,478	4,427,285	647,157
10,597,928	5,157,945	2,313,967
1,504,059	718,792	8,829
2,820,980	1,275,057	50,795
876,203	425,687	38,094
1,519,765	772,760	8,111
737,773	375,638	
144,960,263	76,916,275	6,310,903

By Valeria Olivares and Marisol Chavez

How do people who live near the border on both sides perceive the wall?

Perception about the wall varies among the people who live near it. According to a Cronkite News-Univision News-Dallas Morning News poll that was conducted in 14 U.S. and Mexican cities along the border, 72% of the poll's participants on the U.S. side and 86% on the Mexican side are against the construction of a wall.

Univision News reported: "The wall is seen as a symbol of division and what border residents want is connectivity," said Christopher Wilson, deputy director of the Woodrow Wilson Center's Mexico Institute. "People living on the border feel very connected to the people on the other side."

How does the border facilitate or impede businesses?

Follow this link to view a Hunt Institute interactive data visualization about trends in employment and compensation in El Paso and Doña Ana Counties: https://www.utep.edu/hunt-institute/data/interactive-data-tools/trends-in-employment--compensation.html

Follow this link to view a Hunt Institute interactive data visualization about trends in occupational employment in El Paso and Doña Ana Counties: https://www.utep.edu/hunt-institute/data/

interactive-data-tools/trends-in-occupational-employment.html

Is the proper term American-Mexican border, Mexican-American border, U.S.-Mexico border, or Mexico-U.S. border?

There is no definite answer to this question. The order of the terms is used interchangeably and based on individual preference. However, the first word of the compound term is likely to be influenced by what side of the border the speaker lives on.

Do we need a wall?

This question continues to be highly debated by the public, experts and people in office.[85]

In an opinion piece for Fox News, James Jay Carafano, the vice president of foreign and defense policy studies of The Heritage Foundation wrote, "The president wants to beef up border security. Most Americans share that desire. The wall can help."

Like many other U.S. residents, Carafano finds the wall necessary in order to prevent large amounts of illegal immigrants from coming into the U.S. and destabilizing the country "economically, socially and culturally."

85 https://www.dailyprogress.com/newsvirginian/opinion/guest_columnists/why-do-we-need-a-border-wall/article_b963eff4-0457-11e7-ae51-0b0943e0faf1.html

David Bier, a policy analyst, argued in an opinion piece for the Cato Institute that, "The wall is more than a symbol. It will harm the lives of thousands of border residents and immigrants while wasting billions of tax dollars."

Like other people who live along the border, Bier thinks that the president's proposed wall will be an unnecessary expenditure that will have little impact on security and illegal immigration.

Nora Isabel Lam Gallegos, 26, at the scene, Friday Sept. 7, 2012 in Nuevo Laredo, Tamalipas, Mexico, where her husband Guillermo Arévalo Pedroza, 36, was allegedly shot and killed by a U.S. Border Patrol agent Monday Sept. 3, 2012 on the Rio Grande. Photo by San Antonio Express-News.

A storm rolls in over the Franklin Mountains in El Paso, Texas on November 11, 2019. The riverbed is exposed as the Rio Grande is often dry in the El Paso area. Photo by Aaron Martinez.

Environment

Is the entire 2,000-mile border a desert?

For the most part it is—the border separating the U.S. and Mexico is desert. However, there are bits of farmland, gorges, mountains, a national park in Texas called Big Bend and even an Indian Reservation called Tohono O'odham, not far from Tucson, Ariz.[86] [87]

86 https://www.theguardian.com/artanddesign/2017/feb/23/
cut-in-two-travels-along-the-us-mexico-border-a-photo-essay
87 https://www.cbsnews.com/news/
trump-border-wall-challenge-indian-reservation-arizona/

What are the sister cities along the border?

The sister cities along the border are:

U.S. side	Mexican side
San Isidro, California	Tijuana, Baja California
Calexico, California	Calexico, Baja California
Yuma, Arizona	San Luis Potosí, San Luis Potosí
Nogales, Arizona	Nogales, Sonora
Naco, Arizona	Naco, Sonora
Douglas, Arizona	Agua Prieta, Sonora
Columbus, New Mexico	Puerto Palomas, Chihuahua
El Paso, Texas/Santa Teresa, New Mexico	Ciudad Juárez, Chihuahua
Presidio, Texas	Ojinaga, Chihuahua
Del Rio, Texas	Ciudad Acuña, Coahuila
Eagle Pass, Texas	Piedras Negras, Coahuila
Laredo, Texas	Nuevo Laredo, Tamaulipas
McAllen, Texas	Reynosa, Tamaulipas
Weslaco, Texas	Ciudad Rio Bravo, Tamaulipas
Brownsville, Texas	Matamoros, Tamaulipas

U.S.-Mexico Border Region – Región Fronteriza México-Estados Unidos

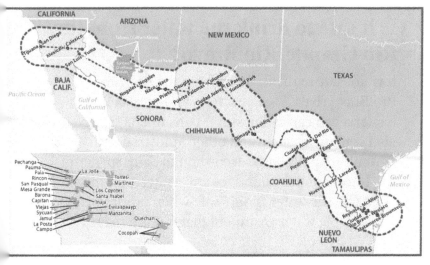

How do the U.S. and Mexico decide on how much water each one can draw from the Colorado River and the Rio Grande?

The sharing of water between the two countries was always an issue until the 1944 Water Treaty. The treaty specifies that the International Boundary and Water Commission (IBCW), both on the U.S. side and on the Mexican side of the border, would be responsible for any issues that arise when the countries didn't agree. The treaty also specifies that the U.S. is required to provide Mexico with 1.5 million acre-feet of Colorado River water, annually. The U.S delivers 60,000 acre- feet of water annually to Ciudad Juárez from the Rio Grande, if the flow of the river is not low.[88] [89]

Is it safe to drink the water from the Rio Grande/Rio Bravo?

It is not safe to drink water from the Rio Grande/ Rio Bravo river. *E. coli* bacteria and fecal coliform bacteria can cause illnesses if consumed. The river also contains arsenic and other industrial and agriculture pollutants, according to Sally Spener of the International Boundary and Water Commission (IBWC). The water is only safe when properly treated at a potable water treatment plant. It is a main

---

88 https://fas.org/sgp/crs/row/R43312.pdf
89 https://www.ibwc.gov/About_Us/About_Us.html

drinking water source for border communities in the U.S. and Mexico.

Can people swim in it?

There are many areas of the Rio Grande where it's OK to swim, but other locations are not safe for swimming due to high bacteria levels. The Rio Grande is impacted by bacteria at and downstream from El Paso and at/or downstream from Del Rio, Eagle Pass and Laredo, Texas, downstream from Falcon Reservoir, and in parts of the lower Rio Grande Valley.

What pollutants affect the Rio Grande?

Bacteria, chloride, total dissolved solids (salinity) and sulfate affect the Rio Grande. Detailed information is available at the following links:

Read more: http://bit.ly/IBWC-source

Read more: https://www.nps.gov/rigr/planyourvisit/riverwaterquality.htm

Why is it called the Rio Grande by the U.S side and Rio Bravo by the Mexican side?

The Treaty of Guadalupe, signed in 1848, ended the war between the U.S. and Mexico and describes the river as the "Rio Grande," which was the new boundary that separated the countries. Rio Grande was a name given by Mexican revolutionaries in Laredo, Texas in 1840. Although there is no historical record of why Mexican people call the river "Rio Bravo," some theories claim that it is a name to describe how turbulent the water was when people tried to cross into the U.S.[90] [91]

Is the air along the border crossings polluted? Is it safe to breathe? What produces the air pollution and where is it the worst?

The air along the borders is polluted and it affects the border communities immensely. The main causes for air pollution are: vehicles, industry, aging geothermal plants, legal and illegal burnings and dust from the desert and unpaved roads, according to Eugenia Posada from the Texas Commission of Environmental Equality (TCEQ).

High elevations of particulate matter, PM2.5 and PM10, which are considered carcinogenic, affect border communities. These cancer-causing pollutants include: emissions from electrical generation as well as other industrial sources, unpaved roads, diesel trucks, buses and cars, especially those idling for long periods of time at border check points. These are all significant

90 https://www.elpasotimes.com/story/news/history/blogs/
tales-from-the-morgue/2010/04/09/1881/31499521/
91 http://www.dallasobserver.com/news/rio-grande-or-rio-
bravo-why-cant-mexico-and-the-us-agree-6426498

contributors on why air quality is at its worst in border regions.

According to this map from the World Quality Website (http://aqicn.org/map/northamerica/) the air along the Mexican border is mostly moderate to unhealthy for sensitive groups. In other areas closer to Florida, the air quality seems to be better. The air quality is best in the middle of the U.S. and toward Canada.[92]

Air pollution can come from a variety of sources that can be man-made, as well as produced

AQI	Air Pollution Level	Health Implications
0 - 50	Good	Air quality is considered satisfactory, and air pollution poses little or no risk
51 -100	Moderate	Air quality is acceptable; however, for some pollutants there may be a moderate health concern for a very small number of people who are unusually sensitive to air pollution.
101-150	Unhealthy for Sensitive Groups	Members of sensitive groups may experience health effects. The general public is not likely to be affected.
151-200	Unhealthy	Everyone may begin to experience health effects; members of sensitive groups may experience more serious health effects
201-300	Very Unhealthy	Health warnings of emergency conditions. The entire population is more likely to be affected.
300+	Hazardous	Health alert: everyone may experience more serious health effects

naturally. Researchers have demonstrated that air pollution can worsen asthma symptoms. Ozone is a gas and is the most common air pollutant. This gas is

92 http://www.aafa.org/page/air-pollution-smog-asthma.aspx

a contributor to haze and smog. It is also triggering to asthma and an irritant to lungs and airways. Airborne particles trigger asthma the most, even in the long term, and are found in smog, haze, smoke and airborne dust. These airborne particles are very small and can easily be inhaled through the mouth and nose. They reduce lung function and can be more visible during the summer.[93] [94]

Are there U.S. and Mexican national parks along the U.S.-Mexico border?

There are several national parks either on or near the border. Some of these include: Joshua Tree National Park (California), Cabeza Prieta National Wildlife Refuge (Arizona), Organ Pipe Cactus National Monument (Arizona), Sonoran Desert National Monument (Arizona), Ironwood National Monument (Arizona), Saguaro National Monument (Arizona), Organ Mountains-Desert Peaks National Monument (New Mexico), Chamizal National Memorial (Texas), Carlsbad Caverns National Park (New Mexico), Big Bend National Park (Texas), Santa Ana National Refuge (Texas), Lower Rio Grande Valley National Wildlife Refuge (Texas) and Laguna Atascosa National Wildlife Refuge (Texas).

On the Mexican side, national parks include: Parque Nacional Constitucion de 1857 (Baja California), Parque Nacional Sierra de San Pedro Martir (Baja

93 https://thinkprogress.org/
us-mexico-border-is-suffocating-in-pollution-4d5e6537f5b2/
94 https://www.epa.gov/border2020/air-policy-forum

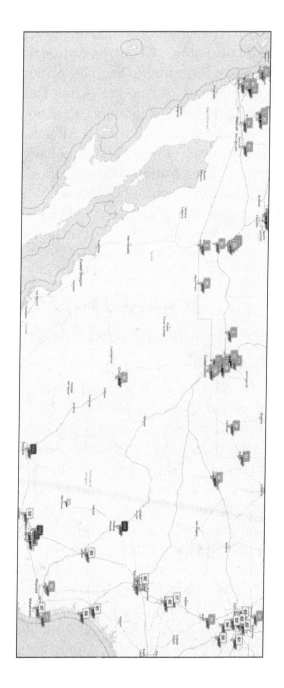

California), Parque Nacional Marino Achipiélago de San Lorenzo (Baja California), Parque Nacional Garden (San Luis Potosí), Gogorrón National Park (San Luis Potosí), Bicentinario San Luis National Park (San Luis Potosí), El Pinacate y Gran Desierto de Altar Biosphere Reserve (Sonora), Rancho La Sierrita (Sonora), Parque Chamizal (Chihuahua), Cumbres de Majalca National Park (Chihuahua), Cañon de Santa Elena National Park (Chihuahua), Parque Nacional Los Novillos (Coahuila), Mendez Park (Tamaulipas), Biosphere Reserve El Cielo (Tamaulipas), Parque Bicentinario (Tamaulipas) and Boca Chica State Park (Tamaulipas).

How can a wall affect the environment's fauna and flora along the border?

The potential effects of a wall are numerous. There are more than 400 species of affected birds, two endangered wildcats, ocelot and jaguarundi, sabal palm trees and more. Noise and traffic are already factors that disturb wildlife. A wall might prevent free movement for animals, especially when there are droughts, flooding or other natural disasters. The Mexican gray wolf is slowly making its way back to Texas. They were nearly wiped out in the 1970s by U.S. residents and in the 1980s by Mexican residents because the wolf was seen as a predator. There are about 120 Mexican gray wolves in the areas of Arizona and New Mexico, and about 30 in Mexico. They are mainly found in Montana and a

small part in the state of Washington. Members of
the Sierra Group-Rio Grande chapter are working
and planning with the state of Texas to help build a
place in the Chihuahuan desert for the Mexican gray
wolf.[95] [96] [97]

Are there river water shortages along the U.S.-Mexico border?

Yes, there are river water shortages along the U.S.-
Mexico border. The main water shortages take place
by the Juárez and El Paso region due to agriculture
withdrawals in which 80% of water is consumed
by farmlands.[98] Population growth is also a factor
that leads to the water shortages, according to Sally
Spener of the IBWC.

Are there drought issues along the U.S.-Mexico border, and how are they dealt with?

During periods of drought in the El Paso-Las
Cruces-Ciudad Juárez area, there is a proportional
reduction to users. In the Lower Rio Grande Valley
in Texas, priority is given to municipal use over

95 http://www.businessinsider.com/
environmental-effects-trump-border-wall-regulations-2017-8
96 http://borderzine.com/2018/05/
mexican-gray-wolf-slowly-making-its-way-back-to-texas/
97 http://www.pewtrusts.org/en/research-
and-analysis/analysis/2015/03/31/
new-bills-threaten-national-parks-wilderness-wildlife-refuges
98 https://www.e-education.psu.edu/earth111/node/993

agricultural use. If there is a shortage, cities get priority over farmers.

Are there any groundwater/basin water shortages along the U.S.-Mexico border?

Sally Spener of the IBWC, says: "There are no groundwater treaties between the U.S. and Mexico." Gilbert Anaya, also of the IBWC, says: "Experts are optimistic that if we continue to conserve water and continue to develop new technologies, we can have a sustainable water supply to meet long term needs (up to 100 years). I don't know or have enough information about Ciudad Juárez. I don't think they are in as good a shape as El Paso. They have more population and the groundwater aquifers may not have as high a yield, but I can't really say for sure. Drought is predicted to be a continued issue in [the El Paso region] for the foreseeable future. Most, if not all, climate models show increased temperature with less rain. Rain events are also less frequent and more severe, and higher temperatures means less snowpack (where water is stored). In planning, drought (climate change) needs to be studied and planned for."

Is solid waste (trash) affecting the rivers? If so, how?

Trash is a problem everywhere, not just in rivers, according to Sally Spener of the IBWC. Given the Rio Grande is mostly in rural areas, trash in not a main problem. Sediment is a bigger concern.[99][100]

Gilbert Anaya of the IBWC says that sediment is a normal part of river systems: "Because of dams, sediment is trapped in areas where it is not needed, other parts of the river require it for stream health. As sediment is deposited, it builds up and causes issues in terms of flood control. Many areas struggle with sediment because of the change in the regime of water storage and flood control and must invest millions of dollars to deal with sediment removal."

How do maquiladoras/assembly plants affect the environment along the border?

Maquiladoras are manufacturing plants that operate under preferential tariff programs by Mexico as well as in the U.S. Different materials, assembly components and production equipment is used in maquiladoras and are allowed to be transported into Mexico duty-free. When the product has been manufactured, it is sent back to country that

---

99 http://www.articles.latimes.com/2009/nov/01/nation/
na-radiation-newmexico1.html
100 http://www.businessinsider.com/r-river-fouled-by-mine-
waste-in-colorado-reopens-for-recreation-2015-8.html

produces the manufactured goods (mainly the U.S. and Canada). In 1993, the North American Trade Agreement (NAFTA) was established by Canada, Mexico and the U.S. This agreement promised to alleviate a number of trade issues. NAFTA also promised to improve working conditions, enforce environmental laws, diminish the high concentration of maquiladoras along the U.S.-Mexico border and to return any toxic waste that maquiladoras owned by foreign countries might have produced back to those countries. NAFTA didn't have the results its proponents promised, resulting in that toxic waste remaining in Mexico, causing damage to the environment. More than 3,000 maquiladoras dot the border along northern Mexico and have created more than 900,000 jobs.[101] [102] [103]

Are there any Native American reservations along the U.S. border? What is their position about the wall and how are they affected?

Along the border are Pueblo Native Americans and Native Americans that live on reservations. Not all Pueblo peoples are from the same tribe. Native Americans make pueblos, or towns, to live there. In the U.S., there are more than 40 Native American tribes who live in reserved and traditional areas.

101 http://www.umich.edu/~snre492/Jones/maquiladora.htm
102 https://www.thoughtco.com/
maquiladoras-in-mexico-1435789
103 http://manufacturinginmexico.org/
maquiladora-in-mexico/

Twelve of those tribes live as close as one mile from the border of Canada and Mexico. There also some that span further, from Russia to Alaska, including the Inupiat, Yunik and Aleut. Policies that govern international borders have affected Native American tribes drastically. They have altered many of these tribes by questioning their citizenship in their own nations as well as affecting culture, security, language, public health, collective identity and the management of resources like water, tribal lands and wildlife. Native nations, for the most part, have been excluded from policy processes along the border, including the 19th century's border-establishing policies to the 21st century's fencing of the border.[104] [105] [106] [107] [108] [109]

104 https://www.npr.org/sections/codeswitch/2014/06/24/323665644/the-map-of-native-american-tribes-youve-never-seen-before
105 http://www.udallcenter.arizona.edu/booksandmore/pdfs/Native.Nations&U.S.Borders_sample.pdf http://www.texasindians.com/tigua.htm
106 https://tshaonline.org/handbook/online/articles/bmt45
107 http://takecareoftexas.org/
108 https://www.npr.org/assets/news/2014/06/Tribal_Nations_Map_NA.pdf
109 https://www.npr.org/assets/news/2014/06/Tribal_Map_Mexico.pdf

Tribal Nations Map
Our Own Names & Locations

Indigenous Nations of México
Our Own Names & Locations

The Rio Grande that flows alongside portions of the
U.S.-Mexico border is a precious source of water
for cotton trees, alfalfa fields and other agriculture.
Joggers, birdwatchers and dune buggy enthusiasts also
make use of the riverbed, which is dry certain times of
the year. Photo by David Smith-Soto for Borderzine.

Beyond borders— envisioning a new Rio Grande

By Shelley Armitage

At first I didn't hear him. Only sensed his peripheral presence.

"Do you know what 'wet-back' means?" he asked.

Now, years later, how could he tug at my memory, especially with those words? Was he a migrant, a vagrant, a fellow citizen, backpack and all?

We stood at the Franklin Mountains look-out point in El Paso, near the famous Rim Road, near the overlook of the river and beyond to the more than one million souls in Juarez. Several people had stopped— laughing, pointing, enjoying a cool early fall day as they peered through the viewing telescopes. Cars pulled akimbo into the narrow parking lot, thread of the river below.

I knew it was pejorative—"wet-back." Just another excuse for someone to say "mexkin," a persistently nasty stereotype for people from south of the border who crossed illegally, but also used to berate Hispanics generally. I'd been taught it was wrong and bit my lip now. I couldn't respond, could hardly look his way, so jarred was I from my tourist bubble.

Then, as if he knew I needed an explanation of the term and why he was using it, he said: "Wetback, yeah. It means the sweat from carrying your brother on your back—across the Rio Bravo, to other places, you know. Sin frontera."

We both looked down at what was more a concrete channel with scant water than a grand river.

Rio Grande, Rio Grande del Norte, Rio Bravo. Since that encounter, I've always wanted to discover your headwaters, as if experiencing your beginnings, middle and end could help explain our complex relationship to you. Seeing the beginning might explain some of the mysteries in between: how the rush of snowpack waters later become mere seeps through sand bars into the Gulf of Mexico. Emerging from the base of Canby Mountain in Colorado, you run wild only there along your 1,896 miles as you serve as a *natural border* between Texas and the Mexican states of Chihuahua, Nuevo Leon and Tamaulipas, and a short boundary between New Mexico and Texas. You pass through (indeed, help create) the two-mile high Rockies, the 1,000 foot plunging basalt gorge north of Taos, the high desert bosque of Albuquerque, green strips of farmland and orchards near Las Cruces, the evocative canyonlands of the Big Bend, the sub-tropical environs of the Texas Valley, until you run the flatlands to the mouth, into the Gulf. And even an area called "the forgotten reach," the mostly dry and forbidding badlands from El Paso to Presidio where you cut a continuous stretch of mostly impenetrable arroyos.

The Mexicans call you Rio Bravo or Rio Bravo del Norte, sometimes interpreted as "angry" or "agitated." Rightfully so, as you were once known for your spectacular flooding when your free, undammed waters churned red, spreading fertile sediment. Perhaps today the name is appropriate to your forced domestication—at least eight dams and pervasive diversion for irrigation and urban use reduce you to a dry bed at least half the year near Las Cruces, New Mexico and beyond. East of El Paso, you are replenished by the recycling of sewage plant waters, the effluvia of pesticide-laden agricultural run-off until, at Ojinaga, Mexico the Rio Conchos River infuses you with fresh waters again. When your channels foam with released water in the spring you are one of the deadliest hazards of the borderlands where death by drowning takes locals and migrants alike.

But to the Navajo you were *Ba'aadi*, "Female River" for your sacred direction. Pueblo people called you *mets'ichi chena* (Keresan); *posoge* (Tewa); *pasiapaane* (Tiwa): all meaning "Big River." And in Towa, you were known as *hanapakwa*, "Great Waters." Antedating the coming of the Spanish by centuries, their names suggests your early condition and a sustainable relationship to it before your total appropriation. Historically, the "great waters" were shared by Spanish and Pueblo people alike during drought and flood times. But when Anglos adopted the English water laws, the "first in time, first in right" provision meant that whoever claimed the water first could use as much as desired.

One way to travel your coursings through time is by viewing Laura Gilpin's photographs made from the headwaters to the mouth. Even in 1949, when she published her photo book—after the earlier plans for Elephant Butte Reservoir but before the enormous Amistad Reservoir—she was able to record what seems today like the pristine character of the river and those lives touched along it. She called her book, *River of Destiny*.

Today, at least in the popular national imagination, you are referred to as "our southern border," site of re-imagined drama and real kitsch. Danger, litigation, statistics overwhelm the explanation and understanding of natural and human relationships. It's hard to get the big picture of "great waters." Years ago, to emphasize the innocuousness of our immigration policy, for example, Guillermo Gomez-Pena, a performance artist, straddled your ribbon run dry, building an altar on a sandbar of memory, sanctifying your fickle ways. For you have continued to squirm out of your borders, frustrating the engineers, politicians, and boundary experts who long to define—and confine—you. More recently cultural geographers have advocated "Thinking Like a River," an ecological argument for the efficacy of water management, preservation—admitting to the will of water.

Rather than border, you seem more like channel to me. The kind that prompts a remembrance. I recall seeing your serpentine past preserved in the surviving bosque east of El Paso. You had changed directions as you have historically done, leaving a hollowed-out area as if Awanyu, the Pueblo snake-like deity sanctifying waters often appearing above your banks, had slithered there.

In the 1930s, the New Mexico poet, Peggy Church reflected on her early life near Puye and the Pajarito Plateau, along the narrow-gauge railroad running snug to the cliff walls where the carved Awanyu seems to move above the Rio Grande waters. She writes of the river in her poem "In Terms of Water":

> To tell about a life in terms of water
> As though all one's life had been
> Following a river
> Upstream and toward the source.
> Or are we the bed of our life's river,
> Its jagged or sandy opposition?
>
> The world, the world we try to live in,
> Would be nothing without rivers.
> Rivers begin with rain,
> Sea water rising,
> The sun, the energy of light transforming
> The visible, invisible
> Dancing of many waters.
>
> Water taking the form of snow.
> Mountains of transfiguration.

Yes, Peggy, you remind us about "feeling" like a river, thinking not enough: sense and reason gone blank.

Paul Horgan has written in *The Great River*, a study of the Rio Grande, of the power of water realistically and in the Pueblo imagination: "Gods and heroes were born out of springs, and ever afterward came and went between the above and below worlds through their pools. Every pueblo had sacred springs somewhere nearby. There was every reason to sanctify them—physical, as life depended on water; spiritual, as they had natural mystery which suggested supernatural qualities; for how could it be that when water fell as rain, or as snow, and ran away, or dried up, there should be other water which came and came, secretly and sweetly, out of the ground, and never failed." Rio Bravo, springs gave you birth and still feed you too.

What would it take to *channel* the Rio?

Ignoring concrete.

To try to become it, I mean, sense its surges and droughts, be a part of its transfigurations? See as the Green Kingfisher sees the first release of precious springtime water below Percha Dam after the long, dry winter?

A channel aggregates—so unlike a segregating border.

I do the best I can following the giant shadow of the Great Blue Heron when the river runs dry. (River runs dry—now there's a hint. Transform it does, changing to evaporation, clouds, alfalfa, grasslands, canyons. Are we not also its transformed composition? The grass become man?) The heron lopes through the air, and, despite its impressive wingspan, laboriously looks for more water. A nearby ponding of wastewater sometimes will do, but eventually there are the fish to consider. At the Rio Grande Gorge near Taos, I scan the dizzying panorama of the river, imaging myself swimming below. I picture the caballeros laughing at us gringos as they cross near Boquillas in the Big Bend chasing down their cattle to return them to *el otro lado*. Or the stories my friend who grew up in El Paso's Segundo Barrio told about the cattle wandering back and forth across the river into his neighborhood. And how, as a boy, he swam without fear in the river— no pesticides, water aplenty. The pebbled mulch of the abandoned pueblos reminds me of your fertile watershed, how everything is saved, especially in years when you don't overflow your banks. Pueblo terraces, irrigation schemes, check dams, holding tanks.

Yes, we need to keep realizing: "water is life."

In 1986, the Rio Grande was designated one of the endangered wild rivers of America with two sections, the confluence area near Taos, and Santa Elena Canyon in the Big Bend, protected by the Wild Rivers Act. These are beautiful places. Places where the tourists go. But what about the little sandbar downstream from Percha Dam? What about the little places in-between only the Snowy Egret knows? What about one of the most biodiverse ecosystems and dramatic landscapes in North America, little known except for those spending time along the river?

In *Rivers of Empire: Water, Aridity and the Growth of the American West*, Donald Worster devotes only two pages to the mighty Rio Grande. But his assessment of the power of rivers, even in arid country, rings true: It is "... mobile, elusive, relentless and vulnerable" in its "fundamental rationality" to find the easiest way ultimately to the sea, he writes. As a basic pattern of life and death, a return to the source of being, the water cycle—like the Awanyu of the Pueblo people—is ancient metaphor. As Worster observes, what scientists have added to this sacred pattern is the notion that the movement of water is unending—an undiminished loop that when studied can serve as a model for understanding the entire economy of nature. Perhaps the most disastrous result of our ignoring the water cycle is an alienation from the land and its stream of life—leading, of course, to more objectifying control.

Today, near where I live in southern New Mexico, the Rio Bravo has disappeared into the throes of water control during winter's regulations. Its sandy channel becomes an amateur racetrack for ATVs and old pickups. There is no awareness that some drop of water has passed here making its way to help sustain, not only our area, but the Texas Valley. As one of the richest biospheres in the U.S., the river's contribution to this fertile and diverse landscape is staggering to consider: a biosphere with over half the 175 known butterfly species in the U.S; a bird sanctuary unrivaled in North America; a subtropical area still supporting black bear and ocelots—albeit already severely endangered by habitat loss.

Tonight, I will dream of the squirming channel and of a young man crossing it. The channel is dry, old, abandoned to a new growth of bosque. But the young man's back still is wet with sweat as he carries his burdens and as I try to channel that final drop of the Rio Bravo—to respect, to recognize its profundity before it evaporates, runs dry.

—Shelley Armitage

Dr. Shelley Armitage is professor emerita at the University of Texas at El Paso. Author of many books and articles, her most recent is the memoir, *Walking the Llano*.

About the Editor

Eraldo "Dino" Chiecchi is an associate professor at the University of Texas at El Paso, specializing in multimedia reporting and photojournalism. He is a 30-year veteran of the newspaper industry, having worked in reporting and management positions at the *Associated Press, San Antonio Express-News, Austin American-Statesman* and *South China Morning Post* in Hong Kong. He started his career at the *El Paso Herald-Post* in his hometown. He is a past president of the Texas Associated Press Managing Editors as well as a past president of the National Association of Hispanic Journalists and a former national board member of the Society of Professional Journalists. He is a founding member of the San Antonio Association of Hispanic Journalists. He was named in 2017 to the National Association of Hispanic Journalists Hall of Fame.

9 781641 800600